Vagus Nerve

Activate Your Natural Healing Ability with Self Help Power Exercises to Overcome Anxiety, Retrain Your Brain and Reduce Chronic Illness, Depression, Trauma and Start to Improve Your Life

By

Sean Back

Table of Contents

Nerve Stimulation) Is Contra Indicatory?

What Does the Invasive Type of VNS (Vagus Nerve Stimulation) Entail?

What, If Any, Are the Precautions That One with the Implanted Device for VNS (Vagus Nerve Stimulation) Should Take?

What Are Some of the Conditions That Can Benefit from VNS (Vagus Nerve Stimulation)?

How Long Does Surgery to Implant the Device for VNS (Vagal Nerve Stimulation) Take?

How Long Does the Battery Within the Generator of the VNS (Vagal Nerve Stimulation) Device Last?

What Is the Use of the Magnet Given After the VNS (Vagus Nerve Stimulation) Surgery?

Is It Okay to Travel with the Implanted VNS (Vagal Nerve Stimulation) Device?

Can I Undergo Surgery While Having the VNS (Vagus Nerve Stimulation) Device Implanted?

regardless of the end form the information ultimately takes. This includes copied versions of the work both physical, digital and audio unless express consent of the Publisher is provided beforehand. Any additional rights reserved.

Furthermore, the information that can be found within the pages described forthwith shall be considered both accurate and truthful when it comes to the recounting of facts. As such, any use, correct or incorrect, of the provided information will render the Publisher free of responsibility as to the actions taken outside of their direct purview. Regardless, there are zero scenarios where the original author or the Publisher can be deemed liable in any fashion for any damages or hardships that may result from any of the information discussed herein.

Additionally, the information in the following pages is intended only for informational purposes and should thus be thought of as universal. As befitting its nature, it is presented without assurance regarding its prolonged validity or interim quality. Trademarks that are mentioned are done without written consent and can in no way be considered an endorsement from the trademark holder.

Introduction

Congratulations on purchasing the *Vagus Nerve,* and thank you for doing so.

The following chapters will discuss the vagus nerve, which, from a historical perspective, is also known as the pneumogastric nerve. The nerve creates an interface with the parasympathetic system whose function is to control a variety of visceral organs including, the cervix, digestive tract, heart, liver, lungs, and uterus. It also controls some muscles, including those responsible for heart rate, speech, swallowing, and sweating. Regarding the heart rate, it deals with the resting heart rate and can mediate its lowering. It maintains the resting rate at 60 - 80 beats every minute. It can do this in response to your rate of breathing. The slowing of the heart rate concerning breathing occurs during the process of exhaling.

Some reflexes owe their existence to the vagus nerve, including the gag and in some cases, the vomiting reflex. After eating, the nerve has a role in satiety.

Regarding the GIT (Gastrointestinal Tract), the vagus nerves cause the muscles to contract to result in the glands within the regions to secrete. Such muscle movements are involuntary.

The vagus nerve plays a role in regulating your breathing.

At these locations, the nerve branches into other nerves. Physically, the nerves come in pairs, namely the left and right sides. Both of them give rise to the recurrent laryngeal nerves, which both ascend between the esophagus and the trachea, and they go in different directions at the neck base.

The branches of the vagus nerve at the neck base include the pharyngeal branches, the superior laryngeal nerve, and the right recurrent laryngeal nerve. At the level of the thorax, the nerve branches into the cardiac branches, and the left recurrent laryngeal nerve. Irritation of the left recurrent laryngeal nerve can result in experiencing voice hoarseness. The nerve also has bronchial and esophageal branches, with the former part constricting bronchi.

The vagus nerve is part of the ANS (Autonomic Nervous

System) of humans, where it's the most lengthy. The spinal accessory nucleus is the portion of the vagus nerve that has its location at its end.

The vagus nerve originates from the medulla oblongata and ends at the colon of the human body. To reach its end, it traverses several body regions, including the abdomen, chest, and neck. It accesses the diaphragm.

The vagus nerve will work to send sensory kind of information to the CNS (Central Nervous System). The sensory message can involve a variety of feelings, including pain, taste, temperature, and touch. The sensory information can either be somatic or visceral. The former term means affecting the skin and muscles, while the latter word means affecting body organs.

The vagus nerve is part of the cranial nerve system, where it is known as the tenth cranial nerve whose abbreviation is CN X. The Roman numeral X is an indicator of its location. The cranial nerves are twelve in total, and some drugs inhibit the function of the vagus nerve in its various locations. It acts as a link between your brain and different body areas.

The vagus nerve can also affect emotions. When one is under a lot of emotional stress, its stimulation can result in fainting, because of its action of lowering heart rates. The effect will lead to a reduction in the blood movement in the brain. Young children and females are the groups most likely to experience such kind of fainting. Additional effects may include losing control of the bladder, for example, when one experiences episodes of extreme fear.

Fainting due to the influence of the vagus nerve can also be due to exposure to extreme levels of heat, standing over long periods, and straining during a bowel movement.

The effect of the vagus nerve on a variety of human body systems is the foundation for VNS (Vagus Nerve Stimulation) therapy. The management can be useful in controlling epileptic seizures and clinical depression, the latter specifically for cases where drugs are not proving beneficial. Research is showing possibilities of its stimulation relieving tinnitus, which is when one hears sounds within the ear, for example, ringing. Some studies are using VNS to help in losing weight. Its side effects include experiencing shortness of breath. VNS can help in Alzheimer's disease, anxiety disorders, and some forms of bipolar disorder, with some using it for treating cluster headaches and migraines.

The therapy works either through external stimulation or via vagal maneuvers. Externally it may, for example, involve the placing of a device to simulate its action on a body region like within the chest. Examples of the vagal maneuvers include coughing, dipping your face in water that is cold, and holding your breath for minimal seconds. Tensing the muscles of the stomach, as though ready for a bowel movement, is another vagal maneuver.

VNS (Vagal Nerve Stimulation) that has its application only during the day is known as VBLOC (Vagus nerve blocking).

Vagotomy involves cutting of the vagus nerve. The operation is no longer advisable though its use was to control the disease of peptic ulcer. Some studies are considering its use in weight control. The procedure has long-term side effects, including developing a deficiency in Vitamin B 12. The result can be a reduction in the production of red blood cell production. The root cause of the insufficiency is the inability to absorb the vitamin from food due to lack of the intrinsic factor. The vagus nerve plays a role in the production of the biological agent. Lack of Vitamin B 12 can lead to dementia, nerve damage, paranoia, tiredness, and even death.

Some studies are showing that vagotomy can half your risk of Parkinson's disease development. There is research that links the nerve with therapy for inflammatory conditions, for example, rheumatoid arthritis. Research shows that the vagus nerve may have a role in controlling memory. The vagus nerve, through the release of acetylcholine, initiates the relaxation of your body, making you calm mentally. The same is a type of neurotransmitter. In this sense, it acts as a de-stressor.

Bioelectronics, a field of medical study, concerns itself with implants that produce stimulations electrically, in this case, for stimulating the vagus nerve. The left side is the one excited.

The nerve has its name originating from the Latin word vagary, which means wandering. The history of its naming earns it the name wandering nerve.

The strength of the functionality of the vagus nerve is known as the vagal tone. Measurement of the condition can be via the use of the HRV (Heart Rate Variability). The measure describes the difference between the heart rates at the point of breathing in and breathing out. High vagal tones can occur in athletes. Individuals going through bed rest exhibit lower levels of the same. Activities that can improve the measurement include humming, laughing, meditation, singing, and cold rinses of the full body.

An effect on the vagus nerve can have a variety of implications given its distribution within many regions and organs of the human body. Some effects can include struggling to take drinks, painful ear, a decrease in stomach acid production, and abdominal pain or bloating. The specificity of the impact can depend on which area of the vagus nerve is affected.

In the stomach, a condition known as gastroparesis can occur with vagus nerve damage. Here, the involuntary movements that support the passage of, for example, food through the GIT (Gastrointestinal Tract) are affected. The impact is incomplete gastric emptying.

The condition can also occur after a vagotomy procedure. An individual suffering from gastroparesis can experience abdominal bloating, abdominal pain, feeling full immediately they start eating, nausea, vomiting, and weight loss.

They may also lose appetite and experience fluctuating levels of their blood sugar.

The vagus nerve is the most complicated of the cranial nerves. It is responsible for stabilizing the nervous system. It has a role in sexual arousal and urination. The vagus nerve transmits sensory information via a pair of bundles of nerve tissue known as the sensory ganglia. These are the inferior and superior ganglia. The former ganglion branches into two nerves. The nerve branches into the pharyngeal nerve and the superior nerves of the larynx.

Within the PNS (Parasympathetic Nervous System), the vagus nerve is the main nerve. Its distribution is mainly below the head level. There are five main types of vagus nerve divided into either the motor or sensory kind. The former comprises the brachial and gut types, while the latter includes the general, unique, and visceral kinds.

The branchial motor type deals with the muscles of the larynx and the pharynx. The visceral motor handles the smooth muscles of the GIT (Gastrointestinal Tract), the heart, and the URT (Upper Respiratory Tract), while the general sensory type, manages the information, coming from the dura, and ear. The unique sensory type deals with taste arising from the epiglottis, and palate. The visceral afferent deals with diverse anatomical areas, including the heart, larynx, lungs, pharynx, and upper GIT (Gastrointestinal Tract).

In pain therapy, the technique of vagus nerve block is essential in differentiating between varying kinds of pain, including head and facial kinds.

The vagus nerve can also undergo stimulation through simple techniques that you can practice in the comfort of your home. Such exercises include the use of the breathing technique, whose goal is to reduce the rate of inhaling and exhaling. The book will discuss how to achieve the same practically. Other methods may involve the use of temperature-sensitive tips that work to stimulate the vagus nerve. Details of how to accomplish the same are in the book. Simple techniques that require stimulation of the muscles surrounding specific areas can also result in VNS (Vagus Nerve Stimulation).

The strength of VNS (Vagus Nerve Stimulation) lies in the connective role the nerve plays between the brain and diverse body parts. Its dysfunction can, therefore, result in negative consequences, both at the mental and physical levels. Its stimulation, on the other hand, can cause relief both physically and mentally. The stimulation of the vagus nerve, therefore, has a dual approach in healing. At the mental level, it can have a positive impact on moods, which may lead to alleviation of stress and anxiety. Its double effect can also prove useful in the development of chronic illness, with the net impact of improving life quality.

It may be preferable to involve your certified health practitioner in determining the effectiveness of VNS (Vagal Nerve Stimulation) for your specific situation. Some medications may interact negatively with VNS (Vagus Nerve Stimulation), therefore, requiring the approval of a certified health practitioner. The experts can also share information on the legal limits concerning VNS (Vagal Nerve Stimulation).

There are plenty of books on this subject on the market, thanks again for choosing this one! Every effort was made to ensure it is full of as much useful information as possible, please enjoy!

Chapter 1: What Is the Vagus Nerve, Its Importance, Its Locations, and Its Origins

What Is the Vagus Nerve?

The vagus nerve is a nerve of the PNS (Parasympathetic Nervous System), which is a component of the ANS (Autonomic Nervous System), the other segment being the SNS (Sympathetic Nervous System). It connects various organs, including the digestive system, the heart, and the lungs with the brain stem. Other organs that the nerve interacts with include the ear, gall bladder, kidneys, and liver, and neck, organs of female fertility, spleen, tongue, and ureter.

Within the organs of female fertility, it plays a role in sexual arousal, according to orgasm. At the tongue level, it contributes to the sensation of taste by controlling it. At the heart level, the nerve contributes to slowing down of the resting heart rate, a phenomenon that can increase in athletes. The result can impact the level of blood pressure. It has a decrease in impact in individuals under bed rest or those in places that are gravity-defying, for example, astronauts. At the lung level, it contributes to the control of breathing via its brachial motor segment. At the kidney level, it promotes its functionality.

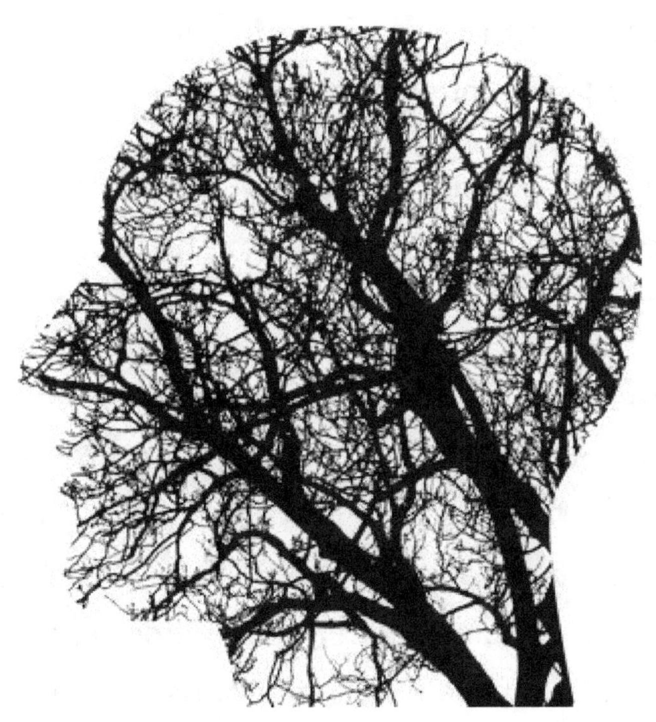

The nerve handles functions of the body that we are not conscious of, for example, digestion. It has a role in balancing blood glucose levels with its effect on the pancreas and liver. At a glandular level, the vagus nerve impacts the secretion of varying biological elements, including bile, saliva, tears, and testosterone.

The vagus nerve consists of five components broadly broken into the motor and sensory elements. The motor kind consists of the visceral and brachial motor vagal nerves, whereas the sensory components include the gut, general, and unique types.

The vagus nerve deals with essential functions that contribute to keeping the human being alive. It integrates with different organs and body systems.

Beyond the physical aspects, the vagus nerve has a role in human emotions. The tie it has connecting physical and emotional features demonstrates why a sentimental influence can have a tangible result. An example is losing control of your bladder when under extreme emotion like fear. The principal organs the vagus nerve coordinates in the emotional context include the brain, the gut, and the heart.

The vagus nerve is also known as the CN X, which stands for the tenth cranial nerve. The Roman numeral component of the abbreviation is an indicator of its location among the twelve cranial nerves. Lengthwise, the vagus nerve is the longest cranial nerve. The component fibers of the vagus nerve follow the Pareto principle, with eighty percent of its fibers, known as afferent fibers, transmitting information to the brain. It acts as a brain modulator. The remaining twenty percent take messages from the brain to the organs. The vagus nerve pair differentiates in direction at the chest level. One component goes to the right while the other chooses the left path. The fibers that make up the vagus nerve number in the tens of thousands.

Acetylcholine is a biological substance that runs through the vagus nerve, helping it to transmit messages.

What Is the Importance of the Vagus Nerve?

The vagus nerve plays an essential role in regulating a variety of physiological functions within the human body. The tasks include the regulation of blood pressure, digestion, heart rate, speaking, and sweating. Among the parasympathetic nerves, the vagus nerve is the principal one. The body regions it covers include the abdomen, chest, head, and neck.

It also plays a role in a variety of reflexes, including gag and vomiting reflexes. It contributes to the cough reflex, particularly when the ear canal gets stimulated. The vagus nerve has a role in the inflammatory reflex. It has a role in immune function.

One of the significant reflexes it is involved in is the vasovagal reflex. This phenomenon comprises two elements, specifically lowering the blood pressure and heart rate slowing. It may lead to fainting known as vasovagal syncope.

The autonomic roles of which one is unconscious of that the vagal nerve is involved in includes mediating the movement of smooth muscles within the GIT (Gastrointestinal Tract). The action is essential in moving, for example, food through the system. The vagus nerve also controls the vascular tone.

Some biological conditions, for example, dysautonomia, can cause activation of the vagus nerve at an excessive level. Stimulation of the right vagus nerve can cause an increase in heart rate while that of the left can lead to a type of heart block.

Appropriate stimulation of the vagus nerve can be therapeutic. The stimulation can either be via electric or manual tools. The former method may involve the insertion of an electronic apparatus below the skin at the chest region. Some devices are non-invasive. One of the manual techniques of stimulating the vagus nerve is known as the Valsalva maneuver. Electronic tools for stimulating the vagus nerve are known as VNS (Vagus Nerve Stimulating) tools. They have been successful in therapy for cases of depression and epilepsy that do not respond to drugs.

Stimulation of the vagus fiber can cause hiccups to stop. The diagnosis of some heart murmurs is via the stimulation of the vagus nerve. The vagus nerve plays a role in inhibiting inflammation. A symptom presents in a variety of disease states. Vagal tone is directly proportionate to the presence or absence of inflammatory conditions with low levels indicating the presence of the disease state. Rheumatoid arthritis is an example of a disease whose prediction can be via vagal tone. Inflammatory bowel syndrome can also benefit from the stimulation of the vagus nerve.

Historically, cutting of the vagus nerve, known as vagotomy, was a therapeutic recommendation for treating peptic ulcers. The reasoning was its effect on the secretion of acid within the stomach region.

An electrocardiogram can measure the activity of the vagus nerve.

Anesthesia can harm the signaling ability of the vagus nerve.

The vagus nerve plays a role in controlling memories and moods. Stimulation of the nerve can aid in PTSD (Post Traumatic Stress Disorder) therapy.

Locations of the Vagus Nerve

The vagus fiber reaches the abdomen by passing through the thorax and neck from the brain stem. It is a paired nerve that branches to the left and right at the position of the neck. Most of its subsequent branches have their location at below head level. The vagus nerve has a wide distribution within the human body. Its nerve components range in the tens of thousands, with some going towards the brain known as the afferent fibers. The ones moving away from the brain are known as efferent fibers. The former type accounts for twenty percent of the total nerve composition.

The components of the afferent ones are the visceral and somatic fibers. The categories of the efferent nerves are the special and general ones. The vagus nerve is part of the PNS (Parasympathetic Nervous System).

The body regions containing branches of the vagus nerve include the abdomen, neck, jugular fossa, and thorax. The stomach area contains the celiac, gastric, and hepatic vagal nerve branches. The jugular fossa region contains the auricular and the meningeal arms, while the neck area includes the laryngeal, pharyngeal, and superior cardiac branches. The divisions of the laryngeal branch are the superior nerve and recurrent. The thorax contains the bronchial branches, the esophageal branches, and the inferior cardiac nerve. The bronchial arms have their divisions as anterior and posterior.

The afferent vagus nerves are also known as sensory, while the efferent is called motor.

The general afferent vagal fibers get information from the external portion of the auditory meatus, the outside and posterior areas of the tympanic membrane, and the posterior section of the ear.

Visceral afferent and efferent vagal fibers get messages from internal organs of the primary cavity of the human body.

Those receiving communication from the epiglottis and palate are known as special nerves.

Brachial efferent nerves communicate with the branchial arches. These include the mastication muscles, tensor tympani, and tensor Veli palatini.

Primarily, the vagus nerve concentrates on the abdomen and chest in comparison to the neck and head. The origin of the word vagus is a Latin word meaning wandering, which indicates how widespread in location the vagus nerve is. It's also known as the tenth cranial nerve, which has its basis as its location relative to the other cranial nerves, as they leave the brain. They do so from the front backward.

As a human develops, the efferent fibers originate from the medulla oblongata. The afferent ones arise from the cranial neural crest. The crest originates from the layer of ectoderm cells.

Vagal nuclei have their location within the medulla oblongata. These are the dorsal motor, nucleus ambiguus, solitary, and spinal trigeminal.

Dorsal motor deals with efferents going to the GIT (Gastrointestinal Tract) and lungs. Nucleus ambiguus handles the larynx, pharynx, and soft palate. Regarding the heart, it coordinates through its branches.

The solitary nucleus will get information from visceral body organs.

The spinal trigeminal nucleus handles information from posterior cranial fossa dura.

The Origins of the Vagus Nerve

The vagus nerve has its origin as the medulla oblongata. The name vagus, arises from a Latin word, meaning wandering. The description is due to its widespread distribution inside the body. The origin is accurate, developmentally, and physically.

The cell bodies of the vagus nerve have their origins as the dorsal motor nucleus and the inferior and superior ganglions of CN X (tenth cranial nerve). They also arise from the nucleus ambiguus.

The pharyngeal nerve branch of the vagus nerve has its origin as the inferior ganglion. Celiac branches arise from the right side of the vagus nerve.

Within an embryo, the vagus nerve originates from the brachial arch, specifically the fourth one.

The fibers of the vagus nerve arise from varying nuclei, three in number. These are the dorsal, nucleus ambiguus, and the solitary tract. The efferent neurons of the visceral nature arise from the dorsal nucleus, which arises from the medulla. The special type of visceral fibers of the efferent kind arises from the motor neurons that make up the nucleus ambiguus.

When arising from the medulla oblongata, the vagus nerve does so in the form of nerve bundles known as the superior and inferior bundles. Some axons emerge from the superior ganglion component of the vagus fiber. There is a meningeal branch arising from the vagus nerve with the cardiac, pharyngeal, and laryngeal nerves arising from the cervical portion of the vagus nerve.

The pharyngeal vagus nerve branches originate from the superior portion of the vagal ganglion that is inferior.

The superior laryngeal fiber originates from the vagus nerve, specifically the middle portion of its inferior ganglion. The recurrent laryngeal nerves move in the opposing track of their origins.

A pair of cardiac nerves arise from the vagus fiber.

They are known as superior and inferior. On the right side, they emerge from the cardiac trunk, while on the left section, they start only from the recurrent nerve. The superior type of cervical cardiac vagus nerve branches has their origin as the superior cervical ganglion. There are small branches of fibers arising from the celiac branch of the abdominal portion of the vagus nerve.

As the vagus nerve emerges from the medulla oblongata, it does so by many rootlets. The specific location of the emergence is the posterolateral sulcus portion of the medulla. The region lies between the inferior ovary nucleus and the cerebellar peduncle.

The records indicating the presence of the vagus nerve dates back to the 19th century. The documentation is thought to have its origins between the years 1830 and 1840.

The other name of the vagus nerve is the pneumogastric nerve. Sensory wise, you can consider the origin of the vagus nerve to come from the organs to the brain. For motor sensations, the start would come from the head to the organs. Anatomically, the vagus nerve has its origin as the brainstem. Cell bodies of the sensory afferent fibers of the vagus nerves have their beginning as the nodose ganglia.

Chapter 2: Type of Vagus Nerve Fibers, Their Functions, and Symptoms of Vagus Nerve Compression

Type of Vagus Nerve Fibers

Vagus nerve fibers are a component of the PNS (Parasympathetic Nervous System) and, therefore, are a part of the ANS (Autonomic Nervous System). There are no sympathetic nervous components within the vagus nerve in the human body. The nerve components of the vagus nerve range in the tens of thousands in number.

Part of the vagus nerve may communicate with the SNS (Sympathetic Nervous System) within the cervical trunk. Vagus nerves are present within the thoracic region of the human body. Part of the vagus nerve fibers passes at a section lower to the aortic arch. Vagal Nerve Stimulation (VNS) involves the segment within the cervical region.

The vagus nerve comes in a pair of left and right parts. These sections have asymmetric impacts on different organs, for example, the right part, has a tremendous effect on the heart, in comparison to the left. The discovery of the differences in function was in the 20th century, particularly the year 1912, with the variances in roles, therefore, impacting the use of vagal nerve stimulation in therapy for different conditions. The branches of the vagus nerve include the superior cardiac and laryngeal branches, the recurrent laryngeal branch, the inferior cardiac branch, and the pulmonary branches.

The vagus nerve fibers can have their categories broadly as the afferent and efferent fibers. The earlier deal with the sensory message while the latter manages motor communications. The sensory vagus nerve fibers account for eighty percent of the total number, while the motor ones contribute to the remaining twenty percent. Afferent fibers move towards the brain stem while efferent move in the opposite direction away from the brain stem. The efferent vagus nerve fibers have their divisions as the alpha motor neurons and the nerves of the parasympathetic system. There are category A efferent fibers.

Sensory fibers, on the other hand, are divided into classes A, B, and C. Each of these categories have differing purposes. Category A deals with motor and visceral information. Class B focuses on input from the parasympathetic system, while section C deals with messages from viscera. The first two categories of sensory fibers are myelinated, while category C is non-myelinated. Sensory vagus nerve fibers are in communication with the cerebral hemispheres. Category B fibers assist in predicting cardiac activity during the process of vagal nerve stimulation. The classification as A, B, or C of sensory fibers has its basis as the Erlanger-Gasser approach. The various categories exhibit varying conduction capabilities with the B class having a speed of 5 - 10 m/s.

Vagal fibers release acetylcholine. The vagus nerve is also known as the tenth cranial nerve whose abbreviation is CN X. Historically, its name is the pneumogastric nerve.

Another way of categorizing the vagus nerve gives rise to a variety of categories. These include the chemosensory, motor, parasympathetic, somatosensory, and viscerosensory fibers. Each of the vagus nerve categories associates with varying nuclei. The nuclei include the ambiguus, dorsal vagal, solitary nucleus, and spinal trigeminal. The chemosensory and viscerosensory nerve categories link with the Solitary nucleus. The motor vagal fiber component connects with the ambiguus nuclei. The parasympathetic portion links with the dorsal vagal nucleus, while the somatosensory vagal segment connects with the spinal trigeminal nucleus.

The components innervate varying organs. Chemosensory vagal element innervates the epiglottis, particularly the taste buds, while the motor vagal component deals with the larynx, palate, and pharynx. The parasympathetic vagal constituent innervates the autonomic ganglia of the abdomen and the thorax. The somatosensory element innervates the dura, the outer section of the ear canal, and the pinna. Viscerosensory, as per the allusion of the name, innervates the abdominal viscera, the esophagus, larynx, pharynx, and thoracic viscera.

The neurons of the dorsal vagal motor type of neurons are efferent and visceral.

The sensory pathway of the vagus nerve that links with the epiglottis is known as the gustatory pathway.

Vagus motor fibers that are somatic have a role in reflexes, for example, the cough reflex. They also manage the reflex arc regarding the heart. They have a role in the carotid sinus reflex. The carotid sinus reflex plays a role in regulating blood pressure within the arteries.

Functions of Vagus Nerve Fibers

Vagus nerve fibers serve a myriad of roles depending on the organ they innervate. The gastric branch of the vagus nerve has a role in the brain's motivation and reward system. The right vagus branch can achieve a rewarding responsibility via its constituent reward neurons, which are part of its sensory neurons. The area it innervates is the upper section of the gastric system. The vagus nerve mediates the feeling of nausea and fullness. The left branch of the vagus nerve is the one in charge of satiety.

At the level of the heart, the vagus nerve has a role in regulating the heartbeat, where it has the effect of slowing down the rate. The net result is a reduction in blood pressure levels. The right pair of the vagus nerve, regarding this function, has a more prominent role at the heart level. It provides nerves to the atrium and sinus node sections of the heart. The left pair focuses on providing nerves to the left ventricle and the atrioventricular junction, where its impact is controlling cardiac output and myocardial contractility. The activities of these pairs of the vagus nerve work to balance out the SNS (Sympathetic Nervous System). HRV (Heart Rate Variability) is a test that can indicate the level of vagal activity present. The test measures the variability in heart rate over periods between succeeding heartbeats. The stimulation of the vagus nerve can help in reducing the possibility of heart failure as it can reduce the occurrence of ventricular fibrillation. Its stimulation results in a cardioprotective effect.

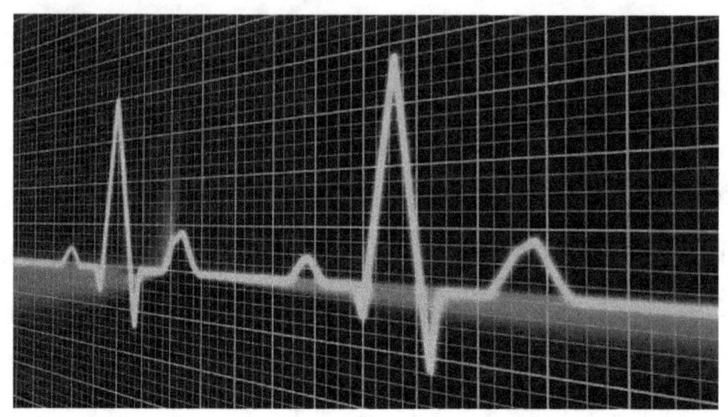

At the gastric level, the vagus nerve works to promote digestion via the phenomenon of peristalsis. It also helps in restoring the human body. Regarding restoration, the vagus nerve assists you achieve a state of relaxation.

The function of the sensory component of the vagus nerve is to send messages to the brain concerning the functioning state of organs within the body cavity after sensing varying stimuli. The stimuli they can sense include chemicals, inflammation, osmotic pressure, pain, pressure, stretch, and temperature. The nuclei portion of the vagus nerve is the one responsible for gathering such sensory signals. The messages the vagus nerve transmits the signals to varying regions of the brain. In response to the information, the brain via the efferent branches of the vagus nerves communicates regulative signs back to organs. The net result is a healthy human body where there is balancing between varying systems. The vagus nerve, therefore, contributes to the prevention of disease states, including arrhythmia, heart failure, and hypertension. It reduces the factors that promote cardiovascular risk.

The vagus nerve can operate as an initiator for the performance of the CNS (Central Nervous System) in the adjustment of limbic and autonomic systems.

The vagus nerve is essential in regulating emotions, including alertness, attention, and moods. Regulation of emotions by the vagus nerve is dependent on the context of experience.

The vagus nerve has a role in inflammation, particularly hindering the process.

The vagus nerve contributes to actions whose basis is glandular, for example, sweating. It supplies nerves to the endocrine and autonomic systems.

It contributes to the movement of the mouth muscles, which in turn aid in speech and in maintaining the open position of the larynx, which is essential for a proper breathing technique. When it comes to its speech function, it does so through its recurrent laryngeal nerve branch. It keeps the larynx open via the posterior cricoarytenoid group of muscles.

The vagus nerve is part of the PNS (Parasympathetic Nervous System).

The vagus nerve controls some skeletal muscles, including the cricothyroid, larynx, levator veli palatini, palatoglossus, palatopharyngeus, pharyngeal constrictors, and salpingopharyngeus. The pharyngeal constrictor muscles that it controls include the inferior, middle, and superior skeletal muscles.

The vagus nerve also supplies afferent nerve fibers known as auricular nerves to the inner section of the ear.

The vagus nerve plays a role in a variety of reflexes, including cough, gag, and vomiting reflexes.

Measurement of vagal reflex can be via the process known as BRS (Baroreflex Sensitivity).

Stimulation of the vagus nerve can protect organs from destruction occurring through the disease state of hypertension.

Symptoms of Vagus Nerve Compression

Manifestations of vagus nerve compression vary since the fiber has an extensive distribution system within the human body. Its compression, therefore, is bound to lead to dysfunction of a variety of body systems. Its well-distributed channels, and therefore connections, means that recovering from its dysfunction can take time. The symptoms of vagus nerve compression link to its functions at various organs.

If the compression is at a point affecting its branches handling the GIT (Gastrointestinal Tract), you may experience chronic nausea. It does this by increasing the secretion of gastric juices, gut movement, and levels of stomach acidity. Compression of the vagus nerve branches dealing with the GIT (Gastrointestinal Tract) can also lead to IBS (Irritable Bowel Syndrome). The condition involves the occurrence of abnormal contractions of the bowel. The basis is the irregularity at the level of the muscular layer with you experiencing constant pains within the stomach in addition to feeling nauseated. At the GIT (Gastrointestinal Tract) level, compression of the vagus nerve may lead you to experience heartburn. Its compression can lead to the occurrence of gastroesophageal reflux.

At the level of blood vessels, it can increase the level of vagal tone, which can result in a decrease in the level of blood pressure. In extreme cases, this can result in fainting known as vasovagal syncope. You may also experience dizziness. The effect of dizziness can worsen when you stand up, especially if you do so abruptly. Organs may also suffer damage due to a decrease in the amount of blood reaching them. When the reduction of the vagal tone also occurs at the heart level, the negative effect can increase.

At the brain level, since the vagus nerve plays a role in regulating your moods, you may experience episodes of anxiety and depression. The depression can also increase in severity if you are experiencing other symptoms of vagus nerve compression, as feeling unwell can lead to a dysfunction of your mental health. You can experience anxiety in the form of panic attacks, especially if you have had an experience of the other symptoms of vagus nerve compression, for example, in a public arena.

The vagus nerve is involved in suppressing

inflammation, or swelling, therefore, its compression can lead to an increase in the occurrence or elongation of episodes of the same.

You may experience a slight difference in your ability to taste since the nerve plays a role in determining the same at specific points of the tongue.

Compression of the vagus nerve can also lead to weight loss as it has a role to play in the regulation of blood glucose levels by the nerves it supplies to the pancreas. The same may occur as an extension of the symptom of nausea. You may also gain weight due to the subsequent imbalance or due to the negative moods of anxiety and depression. Those suffering from vagus nerve compression also report experiencing chronic fatigue that can lead to overeating, therefore, resulting in weight gain.

Any imbalance at the heart level can cause an increase (tachycardia) or a decrease in the heart rate. Bradycardia is the name given to the condition where your heart rate decreases. Physically, such an imbalance can make regular activities, for example, standing, especially over long periods, and walking difficult.

Compression of the vagus nerve can cause you to experience severe headaches, memory loss, and lack of concentration, muscle pain, sleeping problems, and sore throats. All these symptoms can contribute to your levels of chronic fatigue.

Low libido can occur when the vagus nerve undergoes compression.

Chapter 3: Dysfunctions and Inflamed Vagus Nerve

Dysfunctions of the Vagus Nerve

As with other body systems, the vagus nerve can sometimes undergo dysfunction. The extensive nature of the vagus nerve is an indicator of the possible effects of its dysfunction. Its dysfunction, therefore, can lead to multiple organ failure. It may lead to faster deterioration of some disease states, for example, epilepsy, seizures, and sepsis. The dysfunction of the vagus nerve can lead to a decrease in the quality of your life. The basis is because of its effect on multiple body organs.

Dysfunction of the vagus nerve can lead to an increase in the occurrence of inflammation over long periods. The result is because of the vagus nerve ordinarily leading to a reduction in the body's inflammatory reactions. Its suppression can lead to the worsening of inflammatory conditions like rheumatoid arthritis. The basis for the inflammation is the dysfunction of the vagus nerve in its role regarding immunity. Inflammation can also lead to neurological disorders, which can result in cognitive deficits. In severe cases, inflammatory neurological disorders can lead to neurodegeneration. A negative feedback loop can occur when the neurodegeneration affects nerves that play a role in modulating immune reactions, for example, the vagus nerve. The circuit is known as the inflammatory reflex.

Other reflexes that vagus nerve dysfunction influences include the cough reflex resulting in impaired coughing.

Dysfunction of the vagus nerve can also lead to a state of heightened anxiety, which may escalate to panic attacks. The basis is that the vagus nerve plays a role in regulating your moods. You may also experience depressive episodes with an altering of your perception. Those with a traumatic experience can experience more acute episodes of PTSD (Post Traumatic Stress Disorder) if they have a dysfunction of the vagus nerve. In some cases, the combination of the dysfunction and PTSD (Post Traumatic Stress Disorder) can lead to one developing an addiction as a way of coping with everyday life. The cravings can be for medications they are using as therapy for PTSD (Post Traumatic Stress Disorder) or other addictive substances, for example, alcohol.

Dysfunction of the vagus nerve can lead to a decrease in your neuroplasticity capabilities. The result is, for example, the inability to adjust your thinking patterns, which can be essential in dealing with anxiety disorders. The impact can be a prolongation of the effects of PTSD (Post Traumatic Stress Disorders).

Dysfunction of the vagus nerve can lead to experiencing dizziness, and in extreme cases, fainting, and the latter being known as vasovagal syncope. The basis is the reduction in heart rate, and subsequently, a decrease in the amount of blood reaching the brain. The feeling gets worse when you opt to stand up abruptly. Those who have had such an experience publicly can experience an increase in levels of anxiety, both due to vagus nerve dysfunction, and the negative experience memory. The negative moods can have their foundation as the changes in the neurotransmitter levels present within the vagus nerve network. You may also experience a decrease in your ability to focus and poor memory. In extreme cases, you may experience seizures.

When you suffer from vagus nerve dysfunction, you can experience difficulties in breathing. The basis will be the negative effect of the vagus nerve branches that provide nerves to the bronchi. While sleeping, it may worsen a condition known as sleep apnea. Here, one stops breathing during sleep. Additionally, you may experience difficulties in swallowing.

Vagus nerve dysfunction can also lead to blood glucose discrepancies since the fiber has a role in regulating the level of sugars in your body. Its effect on regulating insulin when dysfunctional can be compromised. The result can also be fluctuating weight.

At the heart level, vagus dysfunction can lead to an increase in the rate of your heartbeats, a condition known as tachycardia. A decrease in speed can also occur, a state given the name bradycardia.

Those suffering from vagal nerve dysfunction can experience defective muscle contractions at the bowel level leading to IBS (Irritable Bowel Syndrome). IBS can escalate to toxicity. You may also experience episodes of heartburn and nausea. You may experience symptoms similar to the condition known as pernicious anemia as vagus nerve dysfunction can lead to an inhibition of the absorption of vitamin B12 resulting in its deficiency. The inhibition occurs in the gut. The effect of vagus nerve dysfunction at the GIT (Gastrointestinal tract) can lead to changes in appetite and taste capabilities. Within the GIT (Gastrointestinal Tract) system, dysfunction of the vagus nerve can lead to a condition known as gastroparesis. Here, one experiences a slowing down of gastric emptying, which may cause you to feel full immediately after eating. You may also experience nausea and pain, the latter due to subsequent spasms. Vagus nerve dysfunction at the GIT (Gastrointestinal Tract) level can also cause abdominal bloating and pain.

Some individuals can experience low libido as a result of vagus nerve dysfunction. Males may experience erectile dysfunction, while females may find it difficult to achieve orgasm. Other effects on the reproductive system may include fertility challenges, which may occur due to hormonal imbalances.

Vagus nerve dysfunction can lead to improper balance resulting in episodes of motion sickness.

At the muscle level, vagus nerve dysfunction can cause you to experience fibromyalgia.

Vagus nerve dysfunction can lead to headaches and migraines. It can also cause an increase in the levels of stress, which can create a negative feedback loop regarding the occurrence of migraines and headaches.

Vagus nerve dysfunction can lead to kidney challenges.

A dysfunctional vagal activity can lead to atopic dermatitis. You may also experience your skin tingling or prickling.

Dysfunction of the vagus nerve can lead to chronic pain, for example, in the throat. It may also result in experiencing hoarseness of voice. Your voice may also change.

Dysfunction of the vagus nerve can lead to insomnia.

Vagus nerve dysfunction can cause medicines to have contradictory results for people on particular sections of their bodies.

Inflamed Vagus Fiber

There are varying factors that can lead to the inflammation of the vagus nerve. These may include viruses, drugs, and side effects of surgical interventions, for example, during the insertion of the device for VNS (Vagus Nerve Stimulation). Pressures on the GIT (Gastrointestinal Tract) can also lead to the inflammation of the vagus nerve. Such stresses can come from, for example, overeating.

The effects can be a myriad affecting multiple sites given the extensive distribution of the vagus nerve within the human body. Reports of hoarseness of voice, painful throat, and difficulties in breathing can occur.

Some may complain of a loss of focus, attention, and even memory. Some individuals may complain of mood changes exhibiting anxiety, panic attacks, and depression. Some experience these changes in their weight and blood glucose sugar levels. Regarding weight, both increase and decrease can occur, the former leading to obesity. The result can have its basis as the dysfunction of the vagal effect on satiety, which inflammation may distort. Hernias can also worsen the state of an inflamed vagus nerve as they contribute further to its irritation.

At the heart level, individuals having an inflamed vagus nerve can complain of a variation in their heartbeat rate. They can experience bradycardia, which is the slowing of this rate. When their heart rate increases, they experience tachycardia.

Irritation of the vagus nerve through its inflammation can cause you to experience hiccups.

Various maneuvers can be useful in calming an irritable vagus nerve, including employing a simple exercise of breathing, where you breathe deeply for a short period, and subsequently exhale. You can choose to stop ingesting possible irritants, for example, alcohol, and drugs, the latter of which should involve the advice of your health practitioner. You can take advantage of the breathing exercise to calm yourself down, therefore, reducing your stress levels. Stress can result in a negative feedback loop in the context of an inflamed vagus nerve. Get enough rest to avoid fatigue, which can worsen the effect of an inflamed vagus nerve.

Some maneuvers, for example, the Valsalva maneuver, may require help from a health practitioner to perform.

Some drugs, for example, those containing opioids, can make your symptoms of vagus nerve inflammation worse.

Burping can also provide relief from the symptoms of an inflamed vagus nerve.

Given the essential role that the vagus nerve plays in maintaining healthy bowel movement, supporting this function is crucial. You can do this by, for example, taking enough fluids and eating foods that promote the process can be beneficial when suffering from an inflamed vagus nerve. Proper chewing of food will assist in supporting the inflamed vagus nerve further. The exercise can help you avoid constipation and bloating, which may worsen the state of an inflamed vagus nerve. Avoid spicy meals as they may worsen the state of an inflamed vagus nerve. Caffeine can also further irritate an inflamed vagus nerve in some individuals. The route may be through the inhibition of sleep, which may lead to fatigue, further aggravating the inflamed vagus nerve. Adequate sleep may, therefore, soothe an inflamed vagus nerve.

Changing your posture can assist in dealing with the particular effects of an inflamed vagus nerve like feeling dizzy. Avoid standing up abruptly or standing for long periods, as it may result in fainting. Poor posture can exacerbate the effects of an inflamed vagus nerve.

Magnesium may assist in reducing the impact of an inflamed vagus nerve on the human body.

Experiencing a bitter taste in the mouth can be an indicator of having an inflamed vagus nerve as it has a role in determining how humans perceive taste.

Exercising can sometimes provide relief to those experiencing the effects of an inflamed vagus nerve, including stretching exercises.

Taking control of your thought processes through the process of neuroplasticity can also be beneficial in calming the inflamed vagus nerve. You may achieve such a state through the practice of meditation, which acts to reduce mental clutter, therefore, reducing related stress. The result can be a break of the negative feedback loop in the context of an inflamed vagus nerve, whose driver is stress.

The maneuver to use in dealing with the side effects of an inflamed vagus nerve should depend on the specifics of the impact. VNS (Vagus Nerve Stimulation) may work, for example, in tachycardia, yet may be detrimental in individuals suffering from a reduced heart rate.

You can take advantage of what is known as the diving reflex to calm an inflamed vagus nerve. The maneuver involves dipping your face in ice-cold water. A basic reflex, for example, coughing, may promote calming the inflamed vagus nerve.

For some individuals, singing can be beneficial to an inflamed vagus nerve as it can reduce stress, which can further irritate the fiber. Humming a tune can have the same beneficial effect as singing on the irritated vagus nerve. The scientific basis is the connection of the vagus nerve to the vocal cords. The bond makes gargling have the same positive effect on an inflamed vagus nerve. The actions of gargling, humming, and singing activate a relaxing feeling that can help calm the inflamed vagus nerve.

The act of chewing can also stimulate the vagus nerve, which can be beneficial if its inflammation has led to a decrease in its capability to function correctly.

Given the connection of the vagus nerve with the GIT (Gastrointestinal Tract), intermittent fasting may prove beneficial to providing relief to an inflamed vagus nerve. The action can reduce expectations for its performance of moving food through the tract, which can provide it with adequate time for rest, and, therefore, healing. Beyond the physical aspect, intermittent fasting can promote positive cognitive function, which can counteract the negative consequences of an inflamed vagus nerve, for example, anxiety and stress. The action of intermittent fasting can lead to an improvement in vagal tone, which can be beneficial in instances where its inflammation results in a reduction of the same.

Chapter 4: Connection Between the Vagus Nerve and Other Nerves

The vagus nerve is a fiber that has an extensive distribution network and is, therefore, in communication with a myriad of other nerves. It transverses the body from the brain stem to the second portion of the GIT (Gastrointestinal Tract). These connections assist its functions as it transmits messages to the brain from a variety of organs, and from it to sites where information is required.

Some of its connections include the accessory nerve, facial nerve, glossopharyngeal nerve, hypoglossal nerve, and phrenic nerve. It also interacts with the first two nerves of the spinal cord. The vagus nerve also connects with the great sympathetic nerve.

The connections between the vagus nerve and other nerves can be via ganglions. These include the inferior, inferior vagal, and jugular ganglions.

At the jugular ganglion, the vagus nerve connects with the accessory nerve.

The glossopharyngeal nerve communicates with the vagus nerve via the inferior ganglion.

Both the hypoglossal nerves and the first two nerves of the spinal cord communicate with the vagus nerve via the inferior vagal ganglion.

In some instances, the vagus nerve will connect with other nerves via its branches. An example is where its auricular branch is in communication with the facial nerve. It communicates with the great sympathetic nerve via its numerous filaments. The same is true, particularly for its right branch.

The vagus nerve connects to the ENS (Enteric Nervous System), which regulates the functions in the GIT (Gastrointestinal Tract). It connects it to the CNS (Central Nervous System). The two systems communicate through the vagus nerve. The transmission of messages via the nerve can take seconds.

The connection of the vagus nerves with other nerves, for example, in the brain, can have effects that affect mental states. It may cause changes in moods, for example, releasing the neurotransmitter dopamine, which may uplift one's spirits.

The vagus nerve, through a part of the PNS (Parasympathetic Nervous System), has the capability of activating it via its inherent vagal tone.

Physically speaking, the vagus nerve and its branches may share locations with other nerves as it passes through various areas of the human body. The intricate nature of the positions concerning other nerves is significant with care to be taken, for example, during surgery to avoid affecting other nerves. Though the vagus nerve is part of the PNS (Parasympathetic Nervous System), some SNS (Sympathetic Nervous System) nerves are in contact with it.

The vagus nerve has connections with neurons that monitor blood pressure. Changes in the messages the neurons transmit can determine the reaction of the vagus nerve. For example, if the information the vagus nerve receives signifies an increase in blood pressure, it will work to slow the heart rate. The result should be an overall decrease in blood pressure.

The afferent and efferent branches of the vagus nerve communicate via the cell stations or nuclei, which have their location as the brain stem. The afferent nerves are mainly sensory, while the efferents are motor in nature. The sensory nerves of the vagus fiber arise from two ganglions, namely the ganglion nodosum and the jugular ganglion. The latter is also known as the ganglion of the root. The connection of the accessory nerve to the jugular ganglion is via one or two filaments. The ganglion nodosum is also known as the ganglion of the trunk.

The accessory portion of the vagus nerve correlates with those innervating the pharynx and the larynx. Some parts of the accessory nerve communicate with the sections of the vagus nerve innervating the heart.

The glossopharyngeal nerve further connects with the motor section of the vagus nerve at the nucleus ambiguus. For both nerves, their motor portions relate to the nuclei.

Part of the vagus nerve and the glossopharyngeal nerve seem to end in the same nuclei, therefore, becoming their point of connection. The vagus nerve ends in the inferior part of this nuclei while the glossopharyngeal nerve ends in its superior portion.

The sensory nerves of the vagus nerve at the peripheral point generally are in contact with neurons or muscles.

At the airways, they can detect, for example, irritations, which cause them to initiate the cough reflex. Depending on the severity of the irritation episode, they may cause changes within the lungs, therefore, changing your breathing pattern.

At the diaphragm level, the vagus nerve can cause the

occurrence of hiccups as a response to irritation.

Some scenarios can involve the communication of the vagus nerve and its recipient via the release of chemical substances. These products are known as neurotransmitters. The particular one within the vagus nerve is known as acetylcholine. The material has a variety of actions depending on the focus of the organ or muscle. The vagus nerve can also communicate with other nerves or organs via the production of hormones with acetylcholine playing a role in inhibiting the occurrence of inflammation.

At the heart level, acetylcholine can cause the heart rate to slow down, which may result in drops in blood pressure. Such actions can shift in response to the reaction of the heart following a reflex model as the body aims for maintaining balance through a process known as homeostasis.

At the lung level, the vagus nerve will communicate with the wall of the lungs, particularly its smooth muscles. The recipients of the messages have their location as the bronchial tree. The effect of the vagus nerve is to cause bronchoconstriction, which increases airflow obstruction.

The vagus nerve also communicates with the smooth muscles of the GIT (Gastrointestinal Tract). Here, its branches align themselves between the layers of these muscles. Their specific actions vary depending on the locations within the GIT (Gastrointestinal Tract). The vagus nerve promotes secretion from the glands in the region while diminishing the movement of other muscles. It also works to coordinate the process of peristalsis, which is the movement of, for example, food through the GIT (Gastrointestinal Tract).

At the level of the esophagus, the vagus nerve connects as motor fibers. It connects in the same fashion at the gall bladder, small intestine, and stomach. It has both a motor and secretory function at the stomach level, with the fibers of the vagus nerve affecting these areas all arising from the dorsal nucleus.

The connections of the vagus nerve play a role in the inflammation response. Here, it works by inhibiting the release of chemicals that promote the occurrence of inflammation. The substances are known as cytokines. Their discharge is conditional on the signals the vagus nerve exhibits. It usually occurs when there is exposure to harm or injury. In such scenarios, the vagus nerve will communicate with motor neurons through the nuclei in the brain. The resultant actions of the motor nerves will reduce the production of substances promoting inflammation, and can be protective of body organs. Such a reaction that depends on the connections of the vagus nerve and other nerves can be critical in inflammatory conditions, for example, arthritis. Other substances that determine the extent of inflammation include the TNF (Tumor Necrosis Factor), which is a type of cytokine. Such elements promote the occurrence of inflammatory conditions. These vagus nerve connections can also positively modulate autoimmune responses.

The connections of the vagus nerve to the GIT (Gastrointestinal Tract) can be a conduit for adverse elements to the brain. In the disease state of Parkinsonism, the protein alpha-synuclein acid travels from the stomach to the head.

The connections of the vagus nerves and other nerves can act as a way for the body to make adjustments in a bid to maintain the right balance, a process known as homeostasis. These connections can achieve their purpose as they are the bridge between the brain and organs in the periphery.

Position wise, at the cranium level, the vagus nerve has its location as tenth among other nerves, giving it the name CN X. Its sensory branches interact with the abdomen, ear, larynx, pharynx, and thorax. The motor section communicates with the larynx, pharynx, stomach, and trunk. The vagus nerve also exchanges information with the reproductive organs of the female.

How the vagus nerve interacts with other nerves can affect its tone, which is a description of its capability to function.

The vagus nerve has branches that innervate the tongue, therefore, playing a role in your ability to taste. It does this in association with other nerves that innervate other areas of the organ.

The complexity of the vagus nerve in terms of its distribution can bring it into contact with a variety of other fibers. The connection of the vagus nerve to other nerves provides a route for communication between a diversity of organs and the brain. The information travels in both directions, with each track having its own set of nerves carrying out the communication process.

At the organ level, the way the vagus nerve communicates differs. The connection of the vagus nerve with the nerves forming the SNS (Sympathetic Nervous System) is one that focuses on maintaining a state of balance in the body. These two systems carry out functions that may seem contradictory to each other. An example is when the vagus nerve is working to increase the heart rate that the SNS (Sympathetic Nervous System) is working to cause the opposite reaction.

How the vagus nerve connects to other nerves and organs can affect its ability to function, a parameter whose measurement is known as the vagal tone. The higher the amount, the more likely one experiences the effect of the vagus nerve. The impact of this includes the ability to recover faster after a stressful situation. Those encountering a lower level of vagal tone can suffer adverse effects like a higher probability of suffering from chronic inflammation conditions. HRV (Heart Rate Variability) is the measurement that is in use to indicate the strength of the vagal tone.

Lower levels of the vagal tone will cause the SNS (Sympathetic Nervous System), to compensate for the difference from the point of balance. The impact will lead to, in the case of the inflammation reflex, an increase in the release of substances encouraging inflammation. These substances will act as communication channels between the nerves and the cells. The exchange of information can also cause the discharge of hormones that increase stress levels, for example, cortisol.

Each of these complementary systems is widely in charge of direct opposite functions of the body. The SNS (Sympathetic Nervous System) takes over when you need to 'fight' or 'flee' while the vagus nerve, which is the major component of the PNS (Parasympathetic Nervous System), is in charge when you are to 'rest' or 'digest.

In regards to the glands, the vagus nerve can communicate to encourage the process of sweating.

The vagus nerve can also communicate with other nerves and organs to coordinate the gagging and vomiting reflexes.

In regards to your speaking ability, the vagus nerve is in communication with the muscles of the larynx.

To understand how the vagus nerve communicates with other nerves and organs, you should consider that it consists of cells that make up its two large branches. These cells are the ones that are in constant communication with a variety of organs and other nerves.

The communication of the vagus nerve at the ear level allows you to feel the touch sensation in its inner parts.

At the pharynx level, it handles the gag reflex, also known as the pharyngeal reflex. The function of this action is two-fold, that is, to coordinate vomiting and prevent chocking.

The vagus nerve is also known as the pneumogastric nerve. It connects to the medulla oblongata at the brain level via filaments, which number between eight and ten.

Though the branches of the vagus nerve divert to connect to a variety of organs, at some point, they merge to form a single cord, for example, beneath the jugular foramen. The combination can be for different purposes, for example, to leave together as a single fiber from a section of the body.

Chapter 5: Vagus Nerve and Medicine

The extensive nature and function of the vagus nerve make it an essential focus in medicine. Generally, the mode of utilizing the vagus nerve medically is via its stimulation. Manual or electrical methods are in use to achieve the stimulation. The system in use is dependent on the end purpose that also defines the division of the vagus fiber to undergo stimulation.

Electrical stimulation of the vagus nerve is in use for treating depression and epilepsy, which do not respond to drug therapy. The procedure is not applicable for individuals having undergone resective surgery in epilepsy. It involves implanting the source of electrical stimulation under the skin. The process of implantation requires surgery that may include general anesthesia or local anesthesia. Some scenarios require the patient to stay overnight while others complete the operation within the same day. The length of the procedure is usually between sixty (60) to one hundred and twenty (120) minutes. The devices working to stimulate the vagus nerve then undergo activation by the health practitioner. The patient may get a device, for example, a magnet that they can use to control the vagus nerve stimulation. These devices can assist those who, for example, can diagnose the onset of epileptic seizures. VNS does not have sedation as one of its side effects and does not directly interact with drugs. The latter characteristic reduces its possible array of side effects.

VNS (Vagal Nerve Stimulation) is beneficial, given its low-risk profile, for pregnant patients.

The tools may contain electrodes with the implantation of the device being permanent. The stimulators operate on battery power. The battery power may last for up to ten years, requiring a replacement, which may necessitate a change via minor surgery. Adjusting the equipment depends on the side effects and symptoms. Actual stimulation follows preset cycles with specific currents and frequencies. The pulse width is also a consideration when setting up the gadget.

The procedure usually involves the left vagus nerve. Its stimulation causes electrical signals to move to your brainstem via the nerve. The brainstem then forwards the messages to the appropriate areas of the brain for action. The right portion of the vagus nerve has a connection with your heart making it risky to stimulate.

Some devices can carry out vagus stimulation without the need for surgery. The challenge they possess is their probable inability to be specific in action. The specificity of the devices determines the effectiveness of the vagus nerve stimulation procedure. Such devices are in use to manage cluster headaches, depression, epilepsy, and pain. The instruments work similarly to heart pacemakers.

The devices are in use to support the use of medicines in cases of epilepsy. They can be beneficial in scenarios where you do not respond wholly to medications for epilepsy treatment. The technique can be advantageous in decreasing the number, recovery duration, and intensity of epileptic seizures. It achieves this by stabilizing the amount of abnormal electrical brain activity. Those experiencing focal or partial epileptic seizures may benefit from vagal nerve stimulation. The focus of using the method is long-term as the effects may take months or years to occur. Those experiencing loss of consciousness following seizures may benefit from the stimulation. The concomitant use of such devices and medicine may lead to the reduction of the dosage.

For depression, the procedure may prove beneficial to those, who apart from medications, are not responding to ECT (Electroconvulsive Therapy) or psychotherapy. The approval for its use covers cases of chronic depression. Vagal nerve stimulation for depression can be in use concomitantly with medications. Its benefits may take time, for example, months to years.

Individuals who have attained the age of four (4) can utilize the process of vagal nerve stimulation. In epilepsy, the minimal age for use is twelve (12). The use of VNS (Vagus Nerve Stimulation) for depression requires minimum years of eighteen (18).

There is research involving the use of vagal nerve stimulation for treating Alzheimer's, bipolar disorder, IBS (Inflammatory Bowel Syndrome), obesity, and rheumatoid arthritis. Other conditions where the vagus nerve may be beneficial include asthma, Crohn's disease, stroke, and tinnitus.

Research regarding obesity and the vagus nerve is dependent on the capability of the nerve to transmit messages regarding satiety.

As with most interventions, vagal nerve stimulation comes with risks regarding the surgery and stimulation of the brain. Surgical hazards are similar to other procedures, including difficulty swallowing, infection, pain, and vocal cord paralysis. The paralysis though generally temporary, can be permanent. Other side effects that you may experience once the surgery is complete include cough, headache, hoarseness, insomnia, throat pain, shortness of breath, sleep apnea worsening, tingling of the skin, and voice changes. Voice hoarseness following vagal nerve stimulation is thought to have its basis as overstimulation. Some of the side effects may lessen over time and become tolerable, but some last for the implantation period. Health practitioners may choose to adjust the electrical impulse settings to help you better tolerate the effects. In adverse cases, the device may need removing. Some individuals may experience dysphonia, which is difficulty in speaking. The side effects of VNS (Vagal Nerve Stimulation) may occur due to the stimulation of branches of the vagus nerve fiber that have no relation to the overall purpose of the intervention. Serious side effects of VNS (Vagal Nerve Stimulation) include cardiac arrest. Some individuals may also experience bradycardia and sleepiness. Bleeding may occur as a side effect of VNS (Vagal Nerve Stimulation).

There are particular medications and foods that you may need to stop utilizing when opting for vagus nerve stimulation. Some conditions prohibit the use of the procedure. Switching off of the vagal nerve stimulator may be necessary when exercising, public speaking, and singing. Some medical tests, for example, MRI (Magnetic Resonance Imaging) may affect how the electrical vagal nerve stimulator works. Substances like herbal remedies, OTC (Over The Counter) medications, nutritional supplements, and vitamins may affect the functioning of vagus nerve stimulators.

Stimulation of the vagus nerve may improve life quality and moods.

The positioning of the vagus nerve stimulators depends on the goal of the procedure. For obesity, they have their location as below the belly, while for seizures, the position is the left region of the chest.

Side effects regarding VNS (Vagal Nerve Stimulation) for obesity include heartburn and pain.

Stimulation of the vagus nerve to manage hearing conditions, for example, tinnitus, may not need surgery.

The procedure, in combination with physical therapy, can be beneficial for some stroke patients. Here, the vagus nerve aids in the process of neuroplasticity, enabling a different area of the brain to take over the functions of regions previously negatively affected.

The use of vagus nerve stimulation for treating headaches may not require an invasive technique. Its benefit is for cluster headaches and migraines. Here, the method seems not to possess any adverse effects.

For stimulation of the vagus nerve to be useful as an anti-inflammatory method, it needs balancing the intensity and technique. Most inflammatory conditions exhibit a low vagal tone. Here, its stimulation promotes the reduction of the production of TNF (Tumor Necrosis Factor), belonging to a group of substances known as cytokines. Interleukin 1 beta is another example of a cytokine playing a role in inflammation. Such elements are essential in the occurrence of the inflammatory reflex, a phenomenon in which the vagus nerve plays an important role. The vagus nerve can be beneficial in asthmatic cases as the condition involves the inflammatory reflex. The method may be advantageous for medium and severe cases of asthma. Acetylcholine plays a role in the inflammatory reflex. The function of the vagus nerve in inflammation is proving beneficial in rheumatoid arthritis. Here, it reduces the occurrence of symptoms, for example, swelling.

Vagus nerve stimulation research is ongoing for other conditions, for example, fibromyalgia, heart failure, PTSD (Post Traumatic Stress Disorder), and traumatic brain injuries. Fibromyalgia is an example of a condition concerning chronic pain. Vagus nerve stimulation is undergoing tests for its applicability in handling burns and food allergies.

The use of vagus nerve stimulation is focusing on non-invasive methods to avoid the complications of surgery. Such procedures may involve reaching the fiber via external body regions, for example, the ear and the skin. Apart from specificity, the concern on non-invasive methods is their capability to stimulate effectively. There are wearable non-invasive vagal nerve stimulators available. Non-invasive vagal nerve stimulation is also known as transcutaneous stimulation, with such devices having undergone research for use in depression. The non-invasive tools may require passing them over particular areas of the body, for example, the neck, whenever you need them to send an impulse to the vagus nerve. Rheumatoid arthritis is a condition that may benefit from the use of vagal nerve stimulators that are non -invasive.

Stimulation of the vagus nerve can also be via chemical substances. Heart conditions, for example, heart failure, exhibit a reduction in the activity of the PNS (Parasympathetic Nervous System), which has the vagus nerve as its main component. The use of vagus nerve stimulation to correct the imbalance concomitantly with substances that decrease the sympathetic activity may prove beneficial. Such a two-pronged approach may be the key to achieving an autonomic balance. Other heart conditions that may benefit from vagus nerve stimulation include hypertension and myocardial infarction. Additionally, the anti-inflammatory effect of vagus nerve stimulation further promotes the resolving of heart failure.

The benefits of VNS (Vagus Nerve Stimulation) in heart failure include an improvement in left ventricular functionality, an increase in survival rates, a decrease in the resting heart rate, reduction in hypertrophy, and the preservation of the intrinsic function of cardiac neurons. When using VNS (Vagus Nerve Stimulation) to manage heart failure, the positioning of the stimulator can be on either branch of the fiber. An increase in vagal tone, which has its basis on the reduction of resting heart rate can improve the quality of life.

Chemical stimulation of the vagus nerve exhibits a higher level of specificity in comparison to electrical stimulation. The electrodes in use for electrical stimulation of the vagus nerve have their location at the cervical branch of the fiber. The midsection of the cervical area is the usual location. Lead wires arising from the vagal nerve stimulator go around the vagus nerve at the position of the carotid sheath. Here, electrical impulses get sent to the vagus nerve.

Using VNS (Vagus Nerve Stimulation) in combination with medication, has various benefits, including the reduction of dose-dependent occurrences of side effects, and better control of seizures in epilepsy and depressive episodes.

Devices regarding VNS (Vagus Nerve Stimulation) are now available in the form of RNS (Responsive Nerve Stimulation) tools. These devices have the additional capability of detecting and responding to abnormal activity in, for example, the brain. The focus of the newer models is to interrupt such activities and stop them.

The vagus nerve seems to promote the stimulation of changes in substances known as monoamines in its bid to regulate moods and control seizures.

The approval of the implantation of devices to stimulate the vagus nerve occurs in the 21st century. Non-invasive methods have their consent also within the same century.

There is ongoing research on the possible benefits of using vagal nerve stimulation to manage alcoholic addictions, anxiety, and arrhythmia prevention. The latter may lead to sudden death via the occurrence of cardiac arrests. There is research on its possible impact on neurodevelopmental disorders.

Patients who have previously had neck surgery may be unable to undergo vagus nerve stimulation. Patients with peptic ulcer disease that is active, asthma, are pregnant may not use invasive vagal stimulators. Those having an insulin-dependent form of diabetes mellitus or that suffer from a chronic form of the pulmonary disease, may also not be beneficiaries of vagal nerve stimulation.

Paralysis of the vocal cord may occur with vagus nerve stimulation. Some individuals using VNS (Vagal Nerve Stimulation) report the damage to the nerves innervating the face leading to a condition known as Horner's syndrome.

Chapter 6: Vagus Nerve Stimulation, Learn How to Stimulate It

Vagus Nerve Stimulation

The principal purpose of vagus nerve stimulation is generally to achieve therapeutic outcomes. Its applicability is widening, given the extensive distribution of the vagus nerve within the human body. Medically speaking, the procedure is preferably in use in those who are more than twelve (12) years of age.

Its applicability is in conditions, for example, depression and epilepsy, where there is resistance to improvement from using medications. Such disease states are known as intractable conditions. Its use is also applicable for inflammatory conditions, for example, rheumatoid arthritis and heart failure, the latter having a component of inflammation in its etiology. Here, vagus nerve stimulation inhibits the production of substances that promote the occurrence of inflammation. Such elements include cytokines like TNF (Tumor Necrotic Factor) and IL-1-Beta. Other inflammatory conditions that vagus nerve stimulation can assist include diabetes, lung injury, and sepsis.

Vagal nerve stimulation is beneficial in conditions exhibiting pain, for example, migraines and fibromyalgia.

Other conditions in which vagal nerve stimulation may be beneficial include cardiovascular control, obesity, and stroke.

The branch of the vagus nerve to undergo stimulation will depend on a variety of factors, including the purpose of the procedure. The effects of each nerve branch, are also considered, for example, stimulation of the right vagus nerve may have cardiac effects. It is advisable to carry out such stimulation under the watch of an ECG (Electrocardiogram).

Vagus nerve stimulation provides a pathway through which regulation of the ANS (Autonomic Nervous

System) can be possible. The earliest use of vagus nerve stimulation for therapeutic purposes dates back to the 19th century.

Vagus nerve stimulation may result in some side effects, including cough, dysphonia, and hoarseness. These symptoms may become more tolerable by adjusting the stimulation process. The intensity of the stimulation process is expected to decrease over time.

The stimulation may be reducing seizures by inhibiting the occurrence of abnormal brain activity in areas susceptible to such changes. Regions in the brain that are susceptible to irregular actions may include the hindbrain, locus coeruleus, midbrain, raphe nuclei, thalamocortical projections, the thalamus, and the limbic system. Vagus nerve stimulation can also affect the release of substances in the brain, including norepinephrine and serotonin. Such elements have inhibitory effects on depression and epilepsy. Other areas affected by the brain include the botzinger complex, dorsal motor nucleus, nucleus tractus solitarii, pre-botzinger complex, retrotrapezoid nucleus, and ventral respiratory group.

In refractory epilepsy, vagus nerve stimulation is beneficial as it has a limited amount of side effects.

Pregnant mothers experiencing epilepsy can benefit from the procedure of vagal nerve stimulation. Avoiding the use of drugs during such a stage can protect the unborn child from growth retardation and major congenital types of malformation. The child may also receive protection from developing neurocognitive deficits. Choosing vagal nerve stimulation in pregnancy can help in improving the quality of life of the unborn child. With VNS (Vagal Nerve Stimulation), the child may avoid developing psychiatric and psychological disorders. Aggressive behavior, anxiety, and depression may characterize such disorders.

For children, it is preferable to use vagus nerve stimulation that is non-invasive. Such methods include stimulating the auricular branch of the vagus nerve. The process of transmitting impulses in such scenarios is via the transcutaneous route. Children undergoing vagal nerve stimulation may complain of pain in the arm. Some children as young as two months have experienced VNS (Vagal Nerve Stimulation). Some children may also experience drooling as a side effect of vagal nerve stimulation. The side effects witnessed in children are generally reversible.

The experience of vagal nerve stimulation in children points to the possibility of the benefits of the procedure in neonates. The use in neonates may protect them from the side effects of conventional drugs, including cognitive, psychological, and respiratory disorders.

The discovery of vagus nerve stimulation benefits in depression was through noticing the improvement of moods by those who were using the procedure to manage epilepsy. Vagal nerve stimulation is useful in managing depression that is recurring or chronic. The system operates through altering communication at the prefrontal and medial cortical areas. The procedure may be beneficial for women who suffer from depression post-pregnancy. Using vagus nerve stimulation in such scenarios may prove protective for the infant, for example, for mothers who choose to breastfeed. In pregnancy, the use of vagal nerve stimulation can prevent side effects from drugs, including delivering pre-term and low birth weight. Such medications can pass through the placenta to the unborn child. The procedure may be beneficial to both the mother and the child.

Vagal nerve stimulation offers a widening of choices for managing distress in younger patients who may be prone to side effects of conventional medicines. Even in children, vagal nerve stimulation can cause an uplifting of moods in addition to an improvement of behavior.

The benefits of both depression and epilepsy when using vagal nerve stimulation are usually in the long - term. The periods can be in months to years.

Vagus nerve stimulation can be beneficial in treating Alzheimer's as it has an inflammatory etiology. The benefits may also apply to Crohn's disease. The potential of its anti-inflammatory actions is applicable in both adults and children.

Vagus nerve stimulation can be beneficial in sepsis. The condition involves the presence of bacterial infections and activation of the inflammatory reflex over long periods. The action of vagus nerve stimulation regarding sepsis is preventive as it inhibits the progression of diseases to the condition. The process of inhibition involves balancing between the SNS

(Sympathetic Nervous System) and the PNS
(Parasympathetic Nervous System).

Vagus nerve stimulation has the effect of returning
heightened levels of heart rates to normal base levels.
The overall effect of vagus nerve stimulation is the
reduction of incidences of mortality. The function of the
vagus nerve stimulation of preventing sepsis is essential
in younger patients, who are more prone to such
conditions. Examples of such infections include
chorioamnionitis.

The effect of vagal nerve stimulation on the
inflammatory reflex is beneficial in managing breathing
problems.

Learn How to Stimulate the Vagus Nerve

Stimulation of the vagus nerve can either be chemical,
electrical, or manual. Some of the manual methods
include diving reflex. Here, you splash water of cold
temperature from your scalp line to your lips. The
impact is the cooling down of the nervous system. The

total effect is an increase in the blood flowing to your brain, and slowing down your heart rate. You will get a feeling of relaxation, and you will relieve your negative emotions of, for example, anger. An alternative of attaining the diving reflex is to insert your tongue in a liquid of lukewarm temperature. Fill your mouth with the fluid and try to sense the warmth.

You can use electrical methods to stimulate your vagus nerve through, for example, electrodes. There are gadgets approved for the procedure. It requires approval from health practitioners. You can move the devices over selective areas of your body, for example, the neck, to initiate stimulation of the vagus nerve. Some require insertion via surgery.

Some non-invasive devices are available that work concomitantly with internal implants for better control.

When stimulating your vagus nerve, it is essential to consider a variety of related issues, including the strength of the pulse and specificity of the focus area. Devices with more limited capability for being specific can cause you to experience side effects. The negative impact can be due to a broader range of stimulation.

The purpose for which you are carrying out the vagal stimulation should direct you on the kind of method to utilize. Take note of procedures like MRI (Magnetic Resonance Imaging) that can affect some gadgets in use for vagal nerve stimulation.

Deep breathing is a method that you can use to stimulate the vagus nerve. The impact is at the bronchi level, where the vagus nerve has its branches innervating the region. Here, you need to be conscious of your breathing actions. The technique necessitates you to slow down your breathing to equal five (5) to seven (7) breaths every minute, essentially halving your breathing rate. When applying the method, remember to synergize your diaphragm and belly with the breathing rhythm.

The alternative to the deep breathing technique is by the creation of a constriction at the back section of your throat while creating a 'hhhh' sound.

The manual method that you can use to stimulate your vagus nerve is indirect, unlike the devices that require implantation for functioning. To be impactful at stimulating your vagus nerve, you should focus on the areas where the vagus nerve wanders through. Stimulating such regions will affect the vagus nerve. Examples include the belly, diaphragm, facial muscles, inner ear, lungs, and throat. To arouse the vagus nerve, you should aim to control the actions of such areas.

You can hum as a way of stimulating your vagus nerve as it passes through the vocal cords, making this action effective in impacting the fiber. Humming also stimulates the vagus nerve through the inner ear. You can do this by humming a tune or via meditation, which will produce sensations within your chest, head, and throat.

You could stimulate the vagus nerve through the Valsalva maneuver. Here, your focus is to breathe out while your airways remain closed. To close your airways, pinch your nostrils while keeping your mouth shut. The effect of the technique will be an increase in the pressure level within your chest, which will, in turn, increase your vagal tone.

Socializing can help you stimulate your vagus nerve. The building of relationships can be an avenue for destressing, making you relaxed, which leads to stimulation of your vagus nerve. Aim to reach out to people via varying media, including person to person, phone, and social media channels. Relational actions like hugging can help in initiating the stimulation of the vagus nerve. Healthy socializing can provide you with positive memories, which, when you reflect on, can lead to vagus nerve stimulation. Laughter, which may arise from social situations, can also lead to stimulation of your vagus nerve.

Seeking professional aid can play a decisive part in

helping you stimulate your vagus nerve.

The key to effective stimulation of your vagus nerve is gaining an understanding of how it works.

Singing is another maneuver that you can use to stimulate your vagus nerve. The basis of its impact is the positioning of the branches of the vagus nerve at the vocal cords. Chanting and gargling both have the same foundation for causing the stimulation of the vagus nerve.

Using substances like probiotics can aid in stimulating your vagus nerve. The impact is via the changing of the state of your gut, which, in turn, leads to vagus nerve stimulation. Probiotics can increase the number of particular receptors within the brain, reduce the levels of stress hormones, and reduce behaviors that encourage, for example, anxiety and depression.

You can feed on omega-3 fatty acids to promote the stimulation of your vagus nerve. Such elements support your brain to sustain regular electrical activity. They also increase vagal activity and tone. They increase the variability of the heart rate and encourage heart rate reduction, therefore, stimulating the vagus nerve.

You can choose the route of exercise as a means of stimulating your vagus nerve. The fiber, in turn, stimulates your brain in a variety of ways, including reversing various forms of cognitive decline, supporting the mitochondria, and increasing the levels of growth hormones.

Massage can help you stimulate your vagus nerve. The method can increase your vagal tone and activity. Massaging should be of specific areas, preferably those known to be regions where the vagus nerve innervates. Massaging the foot can increase HRV (Heart Rate Variability), enhance your levels of relaxation, and promotes vagal modulation. Another area that can lead to stimulation of the vagus nerve is the carotid section.

You can stimulate your vagus nerve by controlling your thought processes. Focusing on positive memories can aid in the stimulation of your vagus nerve.

Chapter 7: Vagus Nerve and Hormones, Stress, Brain, Intestine, Immune System, and Anxiety

Vagus Nerve and Hormones

Hormones play a role in the communication of the brain and the gut through the vagus nerve. The impact is on satiation and satisfaction during the digestive process. Such transferring of messages regulates how the human body tolerates glucose levels and energy balances. Communication between the vagus nerve and the organs it innervates may involve the utilization of hormones for communication purposes.

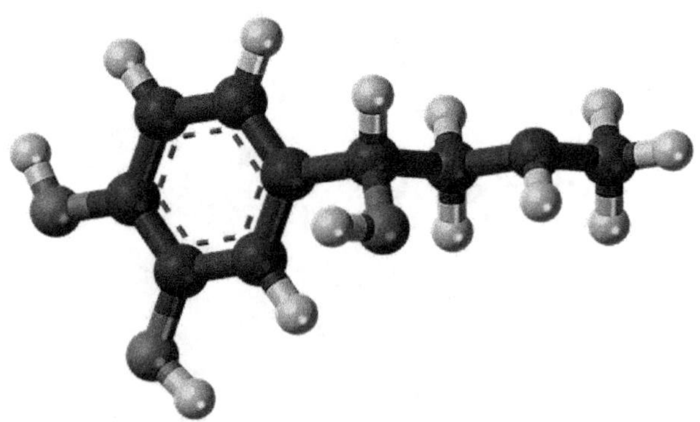

Dysfunction of the vagus nerve can lead to hormonal imbalance. The foundation is the irregularity of messages that the vagus nerve will transmit when it is functioning irregularly. The impact is a negative stimulation of a variety of glands, including the hypothalamus and the pituitary. The functional change from one organ will lead to the distortion in the function of another, therefore, leading to the establishment of a negative feedback loop. Adrenal glands can get affected. The example here is the HPA axis that involves the various organs. In such scenarios, the body t overproduces or reduces its production of hormones. Some of the hormones whose levels of production can change include ACTH (Adrenocorticotropic hormone) and cortisol. The change can produce a phenomenon known as adrenal fatigue. Some of the physical effects can include anxiety and lack of sleep.

Hormonal imbalance due to vagus nerve dysfunction can also affect other systems, including your reproductive organs.

Stimulation of the vagus nerve can lead to the production of some hormones, for example, oxytocin, which can undergo production during the activity of singing, an action that leads to vagus nerve stimulation. Laughter can cause your body to produce substances known as endorphins through the stimulation of the vagus nerve. The activity also leads to the release of an element known as nitric oxide, which can cause the relaxation of muscles lining the blood vessels within your body. The result is, therefore, improving your blood flow.

Serotonin is a substance that is known to stimulate the vagus nerve. It acts as a communication bridge between sets of nerves. The stimulation is at varying points in the human body, including the gut and brain.

Vagus Nerve and Stress

Stimulation of the vagus nerve is known to encourage the body to relax, therefore, allowing you to de-stress. Those who have undergone vagus nerve stimulation may experience positive moods. Vagus nerve stimulation decreases both emotional and physical stress. The vagus nerve is a transmitter of messages to your brain acts to let it know when, for example, your organs undergo stress. Such scenarios can occur, for example, when you experience physical trauma.

The vagus nerve can, for example, reduce the production of the stress hormone cortisol as a way of reducing the negative emotion. It also inhibits the production of adrenaline whose production increases in scenarios requiring you to take a fight or flight decision. The intervention by the vagus nerve will encourage your body to rest. The vagus nerve will promote the production of the substance known as acetylcholine to achieve a state of relaxation. The physical effects of this substance include reducing your blood pressure and heart rate.

The vagal tone, whose measurement is via HRV (Heart Rate Variability), can be an indicator of emotional health. A lower level may indicate an increase in stress levels and vice versa. Working on your vagal tone can, therefore, help you manage your stress levels.

You can increase your vagal tone by stimulating your vagus nerve via a variety of maneuvers. The actions you can take include the practice of deep breathing. Here, you aim to lower your breathing rate to at least half of the regular amount per minute. You can also stimulate your vagus nerve to reduce your stress levels by splashing cold water onto your face. Humming and singing can also help you spur your vagus nerve whenever you feel stressed. You can also opt to meditate as a way of exciting your vagus nerve for destressing purposes.

Laughing is a proven method for stimulating your vagus nerve. Developing healthy relationships can act as a route of destressing and may even support an environment that encourages laughter. Intermittent fasting can also aid your goal of vagus nerve stimulation for destressing purposes.

Vagus Nerve and Brain

Anatomically speaking, the vagus nerve descends from the brain stems to the various body parts. Communication at the brain level requires the vagus nerve to produce neurotransmitters. These are substances that carry information between nerves. The element that the vagus nerve uses is known as acetylcholine. It promotes a variety of actions depending on the organ it wants to regulate.

The actions of the vagus nerve within the brain play a role in maintaining emotional stability. Its activities may keep negative feelings like anxiety and depression at bay. Here, the stimulation method of choice can either be chemical, electrical, or physical.

The electrical route requires a surgical operation for implantation. The option may take some time for its effects to exhibit, for example, months or years.

Chemically, the vagus nerve transports specific biological substances to the brain from a variety of organs, for example, the gut, therefore, regulating mental health. Changes in the physical structure of, for example, the stomach can induce the vagus nerve to encourage positive reactions from the brain.

These effects of the vagus nerve on the brain can promote the management and treatment of some psychiatric disorders. The extensive nature of the vagus nerve and its connection to the head can give it the power to determine how you feel. It defines the extent to which you experience varying symptoms. Its stimulation can, for example, reduce how you experience the effects of autism. Its connection with the brain is also critical in the period of recovering from a stroke. Here, its stimulation can support the brain's capacity to heal itself after the traumatic event.

Stimulation of the vagus nerve can allow it to promote a balance within the ANS (Autonomic Nervous System). The vagus nerve is, therefore, a bridge between a variety of body organs and the brain.

Vagus Nerve and Intestine

The vagus nerve plays an essential role in the gut-brain axis. Its dysfunction can lead to the development of a variety of conditions, including IBS (Irritable Bowel Syndrome), a type of IBD (Inflammatory Bowel Disease). At the intestine level, it is responsible for promoting the phenomenon of peristalsis. When the vagal tone decreases, the effect at the intestine level can include the occurrence of inflammation. The basis of the impact is the role the vagus nerve plays in the inflammatory reflex. Other conditions that may develop at the intestinal level due to a dysfunction of the vagus nerve include Crohn's disease.

The symptoms that arise when there is vagus nerve dysfunction at the intestinal level include abdominal pain, weight loss, fever, and diarrhea. The overall effect is a reduction in life quality for those experiencing vagus nerve dysfunction. The role of the vagus nerve in the gut-brain axis gets support from its function at the neuro-endocrine-immune axis. The vagus nerve can utilize the latter axis to balance out any negative consequences occurring at the gut level. Its stimulation can lead to an improvement in colitis, which is the inflammation of the colon, a section of the large intestines.

The vagus nerve can also reduce inflammation at the intestine level via the cholinergic pathway. Vagus nerve stimulation inhibits the production of substances that promote inflammation, for example, cytokines like alpha-TNF (Tumor Necrotic Factor).

Stimulation of the vagus nerve at the intestine level can be via the introduction of chemical substances, for example, nicotine. The GIT (Gastrointestinal Tract) of which, the intestine is a part, has interaction with several vagus nerve branches.

At the intestine level, the vagus nerve interacts with the ENS (Enteric Nervous System). The vagus nerve has a role in digestion and food intake at the intestine level. It also plays a part in communicating satiety to the brain via its receptors at the intestine. The messages the vagus nerve transmits from here can lead to the release of a variety of biological substances, including gastric acid, glucagon, and insulin. The stimulation of the vagus nerve causes the levels of these substances to increase. It also affects the barrier of the intestines. Vagus nerve stimulation at the intestine level can either be physical, for example, through the process of enlargement or chemical.

Vagus Nerve and Immune System

The role of the vagus nerve in the inflammatory reflex is an indicator of its function in the immune system. It can determine the release of substances that modulate the immune system, including cytokines. Examples of the cytokines include TNF (Tumor Necrotic Factor) and IL-6 (Interleukin 6). The production of such substances in the body can lead to the release of other elements that further promote the response of the immune system. It utilizes neurotransmitters to regulate the same. The function of the vagus nerve in immunity comes into play when the body is under attack from pathogens. Its role is also observable when your tissues undergo injury. These injuries or pathogens are the ones that cause the initiation of the immune response, which the vagus nerve regulates. Given the role of the vagus nerve in the immune response, its dysfunction can lead to the pathophysiology of various body systems.

The vagus nerve works to maintain homeostasis within the immune system in conjunction with the SNS (Sympathetic Nervous System). The interaction of these two systems is via the splenic nerve. The afferent fibers of the vagus nerve deal with the glandular responses of the immune system while the efferent ones handle the neurotransmitter response.

Stimulation of the vagus nerve can cause result in the

regulation of the immune system. This capability allows the vagus nerve to be beneficial in managing autoimmune disorders, for example, Crohn's disease, lupus, and rheumatoid arthritis. Stimulating the vagus nerve in such conditions can be via electrical stimulation. The devices in use for the process are known as electroceuticals. The spleen plays an essential role in the connection between the vagus nerve and the immune system. Activation of the vagus nerve leads to the transmission of information to the spleen, which regulates immune cells. In such a setting, the immune cells behave like neurons with the communication between them and nerves being via synapses. The stimulation of the cells within the spleen causes them to release the neurotransmitter that is present within the efferent branches of the vagus nerve. The chemical substance is known as acetylcholine.

Vagus Nerve and Anxiety

The vagus nerve plays a role in determining your moods. Its stimulation can cause you to feel relaxed and at rest, while its dysfunction may lead to the development of feelings of anxiety. Severe cases can develop into fear and even panic attacks. Stimulation of the vagus nerve can, therefore, reduce worry.

During emotional episodes, the afferent arm of the vagus nerve via beta-adrenergic receptors can detect the release of norepinephrine. This neurotransmitter release occurs when the body is embracing a fight or flight response. The chemical substance has a role in creating memories that associate with the happenings that promote the said response. The efferent branch of the vagus nerve will fight the reaction by enhancing moods and reducing anxiety. Stimulation of the vagus nerve to allay fear can be via its electrical stimulation. The advantage of the same is its lack of side effects, usually concerning pharmaceutical components in use for anxiety attacks.

Vagus nerve stimulation can work well for anxiety disorders that do not respond to pharmaceutical agents. The procedure may be in use concurrently with pharmaceuticals on advice from qualified health practitioners. Adjustments to the device can occur until the establishment of a suitable cycle. The advantage of vagal nerve stimulation regarding anxiety is its two-pronged action as it deals with fear and anxiety concurrently. It can, therefore, be beneficial for severe cases of anxiety disorders. Here, vagal nerve stimulation works to promote cognitive behavioral changes that diminish the impact of anxiety.

Chapter 8: Vagus Nerve and Chronic Illness

The connection of the vagus nerve with a variety of body organs allows it to act as an indicator of overall health. It may indicate the development of chronic illness as well as regulate its exhibition. These illnesses may be mental as well as physical. Chronic diseases that may have a relation to the state of the vagus nerve include autoimmune states. Examples include Crohn's disease, lupus, IBS (Irritable Bowel Syndrome), IBD (Irritable Bowel Diseases), and rheumatoid arthritis. Gastroparesis may also arise from the dysfunction of the vagus nerve.

The vagus nerve usually has a role in chronic non-communicable illnesses. Its function in such diseases ties to its role as a bridge between neural and immune systems. The vagus nerve, therefore, plays an essential role in determining the global burden of disease. The function of the vagus nerve in the inflammation reflex is critical in the contribution of a variety of diseases, including cardiovascular conditions.

On the other hand, the nerve can promote the prevention and probably treatment of such conditions. The vagus nerve being part of the PNS (Parasympathetic Nervous System) can help to create a balance within the ANS (Autonomic Nervous System). The lack of balance can lead to the development of chronic conditions, for example, due to an increase in sympathetic activity. Such actions can result from the SNS (Sympathetic Nervous System), which is also a component of the ANS (Autonomic Nervous System).

The neural part of the vagus nerve functions includes regulating how particular areas of the brain, for example, the frontal area, works. This section is essential in determining the habits that may promote behaviors that support the occurrence of chronic illnesses.

The vagus nerve plays a role in preventing the occurrence of oxidative stress, which is a determinant of the development of chronic illnesses. The vagus nerve can inhibit hypoxia, which can occur in some chronic diseases. Hypoxia may lead to oxidative stress under particular conditions, which is a factor that leads to the development of chronic illnesses.

The vagus nerve can undergo stimulation via non-invasive means to modulate symptoms of chronic illnesses. The phenomenon can occur through the use of electroceuticals. Chronic diseases that may benefit from the stimulation of the vagus nerve include cancer, diabetes, myocardial infarction, and stroke. The positive effect of VNS (Vagus Nerve Stimulation) on these conditions lies in their similarities in biological dysfunctions. The higher the activity of the vagal nerve, the lower the occurrence of chronic diseases.

Psychosocial stress can result in chronic illnesses. The vagus nerve being part of the ANS (Autonomic Nervous System) that encourages rest, can help alleviate such factors. During such scenarios, there may be the production of substances that promote inflammation, which is a factor leading to chronic illnesses. Examples of the elements leading to inflammation include cytokines. Vagus nerve stimulation can lead to a reduction in the production of such components.

The principal underlying reasons leading to chronic illnesses include inflammation, oxidative stress, and an increase in the level of SNS (Sympathetic Nervous

System) activity. Stimulation of the vagus nerve can help negate the effects of these factors.

An increase in SNS (Sympathetic Nervous System) action can cause chronic illnesses within the cardiovascular system. It achieves the disease states by, for example, demanding higher levels of oxygen. The result is a greater work demand from the heart. Persistent order for the organ can lead to its failure. Elevated SNS (Sympathetic Nervous System) activity can also result in the constriction of blood vessels. Such actions further complicate the need for higher levels of oxygen occurring due to a heightened activity level from the SNS (Sympathetic Nervous System). Such activity levels can also complicate chronic illnesses like diabetes.

An increase in the levels of vagus nerve activity can lead to a better recovery from changes in cardiac, hormonal, and inflammatory markers, which ordinarily can cause chronic illnesses. In such scenarios, the function of the vagus nerve is to maintain a balance, a state known as homeostasis. The activity of the vagus nerve can indicate the prognosis of chronic illness.

Studies show that high levels of vagal nerve activity can indicate a lower risk of death from cancer. Regarding diabetes, a higher level of action from the vagus nerve can lead to a lower level of resistance to insulin, an underlying factor in the development of the disease. The inverse relation can undergo measurement by focusing on the levels of HbA1c, an indicator for the average levels of blood glucose over a period.

Measurement of vagal nerve activity can be via ECG (Electrocardiogram), which may predict the occurrence of chronic illnesses and necessitate taking preventive measures. Finger pulse tools are also beneficial in measuring HRV (Heart Rate Variability), which is a direct indicator of the activity levels of the vagus nerve.

Regarding inflammation underlying chronic conditions, the vagus nerve transmits information to the brain on the presence of biological agents that promote inflammation. Such elements include the cytokine known as interleukin-1. The vagus nerve contains receptors that can sense its presence. Here, it is carrying out its function within the immune system by modulating the neural pathways.

The vagus nerve can inhibit the process of inflammation through a two-pronged pathway. It can lead to an increase of cortisol secretion, a hormone that rises when one is under stress. The result is a decrease in the levels of inflammation. It can achieve this via activation of a variety of glands, including the adrenal gland, hypothalamus, and pituitary glands. It can also inhibit inflammation via the splenic pathway. In the second approach, it aims to prevent the formation of biological substances that cause inflammation. The anti-inflammatory reflex of the vagus nerve has these pathways as its constituents.

The vagus nerve can induce vasodilation. The net effect is the negation of the effects of oxidative stress. An increase in vasodilation levels will cause an increase in blood flow. Examples of chronic illnesses, which can develop when there is a lack of oxygen, include cancer, CHD (Congestive Heart Disease), and stroke.

The principal causes of chronic illness, that is, inflammation, oxidative stress, and heightened sympathetic activity, can also form a negative feedback loop among themselves. The interconnection allows the vagus nerve to have an impact on all the factors concurrently.

Beyond these factors, the vagus nerve can also influence lifestyles that may lead to the development of chronic diseases. The effect of behaviors on the vagus nerve can change its indicator, that is, the HRV (Heart Rate Variability). Those who smoke, for example, have a lower HRV than those who abstain from smoking. The vagus nerve has an influence over lifestyle behaviors via the process of executive functioning. The process involves inhibition, memory, problem-solving, and self-regulation. It positively correlates with HRV. The capability allows the making of choices that do not support the development of chronic illnesses. Examples of negative behaviors that executive function can inhibit include inactivity, smoking, and unhealthy diets.

Vagus nerve stimulation can lead to better emotional control, which, in turn, can inhibit the adoption of behaviors promoting the development of chronic conditions. Its stimulation can, therefore, reduce the occurrences of, for example, emotional eating. The net effect can be weight loss, which can reduce the possibility of developing some chronic illnesses. Vagus nerve stimulation can also reduce food cravings. The control can help in making better decisions regarding diet, which can have a positive effect on preventing the occurrence of chronic illnesses. Some actions that stimulate the vagus nerve, for example, exercising, also have a positive impact on factors that prevent chronic diseases.

Vagal nerve stimulation has a double effect on chronic diseases because it can be beneficial in preventing as well as treating some prolonged ailments. Stimulation of the vagus nerve can be chemical, electrical, or manual. Electrical stimulation can either need surgery, be transcutaneous, or be non-invasive. The less invasive the method, the less likely you have to deal with some side effects, for example, infections after surgery. The challenge with some non-invasive methods of vagus nerve stimulation is the lack of specificity, which can cause the activation of unwanted areas. The result can be a myriad of side effects, which may discourage its use, or a reduction in its efficiency to stimulate the vagus nerve.

Some chronic illnesses that non-invasive devices can manage include depression, inflammation, and prolonged headaches. They may also reduce the amount of glucose in the blood as well as those of HbA1c. The latter is an indicator of long-term blood sugar control.

Manual methods of stimulating the vagus nerve include controlling your breathing manually. The focus here is to reduce it to at least half the regular rate per minute. The action can lead to a reduction in inflammation, for example, in those experiencing hypertension, which is a type of chronic illness. The maneuver can work to reduce some cancer biomarkers, for example, in colon cancer.

The effect of vagus nerve stimulation is usually in the long-term.

You can also use varying forms of meditation to stimulate your vagus nerve as a means of managing chronic illnesses. Some can be in use concurrently with conventional medication. The capability of the vagus nerve has led to the development of anti-inflammatory drugs whose action depends on the fiber. Such substances can be beneficial in cancer where they increase the sensitivity of unwanted growths to, for example, radiotherapy. The developments may aid the management of aggressive forms of cancer.

The vagus nerve can also undergo stimulation via the use of intravenous methods. Such interventions can help in recovery from chronic conditions, for example, myocardial infarction. Recovery from chronic illnesses like a stroke can be faster with the utilization of vagus nerve stimulation.

When stimulating the vagus nerve, it is essential not to

overexcite the fiber, as it may have detrimental effects, including fainting. Overstimulation can also lead to the stopping of the heartbeat. In some cases, it may promote the occurrence or progression of cancer. The focus should be on safety with the stimulation best done in conjunction with qualified health practitioners.

Regarding inflammation, the vagus nerve in use is usually the left branch.

The vagus nerve can show dysfunction when it undergoes infection, for example, by viruses. The vagus nerve plays an essential role in the pathologies that may occur within the GIT (Gastrointestinal Tract). The vagus nerve can undergo stimulation via targeting through the use of enteral nutrition. The chronic condition postoperative ileus may benefit from the stimulation of the vagus nerve. The presence of an imbalance within the vagus nerve can work as an indicator of the possibility of developing chronic neuro-immune disorders. The dysfunction can also be a consequence of such chronic conditions. Vagus nerve stimulation can help relieve chronic pain. Complementary medicine has a role in stimulating the vagus nerve for the relief of chronic disease symptoms.

At the secretory level, the vagus nerve can stimulate the production of ACTH (Adrenocorticotropic Hormone) from the pituitary to prevent inflammation at the periphery. Vagus nerve stimulation can improve the life quality of those suffering from chronic conditions. Stimulating the vagus nerve through meditation can reduce the heart rate, which is essential in some chronic illnesses.

Vagus nerve stimulation may be beneficial in the management of COPD (Chronic Obstructive Pulmonary Disease). The net effect of vagal nerve stimulation is the capability to neuromodulate health. Its stimulation may lead to a reversal of the occurrence of chronic illnesses.

In regards to inflammation, vagus nerve stimulation is powerful in that it hinders the production of substances that undergo production whenever the body experiences stimulation that should result in inflammation. The process can be beneficial in a variety of gut inflammation conditions. The nerve produces a substance to transmit the messages, known as acetylcholine. Stimulation of the vagus nerve can prove useful in kidney conditions whose underlying cause is ischemia. The method can be beneficial even in juveniles with the non-invasive vagus stimulation being preferable for this age set. At the least, vagus nerve stimulation is advantageous in diminishing the symptoms that associate with chronic illnesses.

Chapter 9: Vagus Nerve Malfunctions and How to Use It to Regenerate Your Body

Vagus Nerve Malfunctions

The indicators of vagus nerve malfunction can be many due to its extensive distribution within the body. It runs from the brain stem to the large intestines. The nerve is bi-directional, carrying messages to and from the brain within which the fiber affects varying regions.

The vagus nerve can malfunction due to vagotomy, a procedure involving cutting off the fiber. The same may occur due to trauma or via surgery.

Overstimulation of the vagus nerve can also lead to its malfunction, with the impact sometimes becoming fatal, for example, by causing stopping of the heartbeat.

The symptoms of a malfunctioning vagus nerve can include an increase in sympathetic activity, which may have devastating effects. The vagus nerve, which is part of the PNS (Parasympathetic Nervous System), is a critical component of attaining balance within the body. The process of achieving balance is known as homeostasis. The system and SNS (Sympathetic Nervous System) work in opposite directions to accomplish the situation. The malfunctioning of one system can cause the other to over-function, which can harm the human body. The vagus nerve is the most substantial component of the PNS (Parasympathetic Nervous System), making its optimal function essential for the balance to occur.

Vagus nerve malfunction can also lead to dysfunction of the metabolic system, which may exhibit an increase in the blood sugar levels, a key symptom of diabetes.

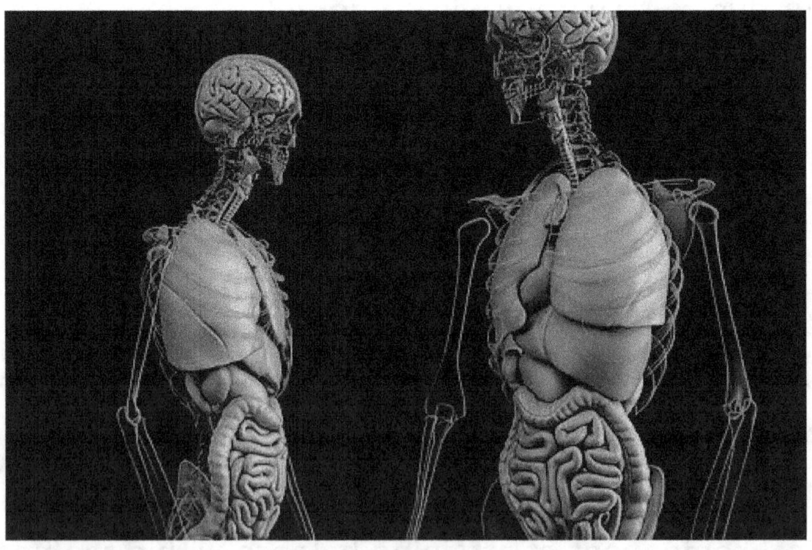

Several symptoms of vagus nerve dysfunction occur at the gut level as the fiber connects this area of the body to the brain.

Heart rates and breathing can undergo a negative impact when the vagus nerve is malfunctioning.

The vagus nerve has a role in inflammation via the inflammatory reflex. Its malfunction can, therefore, lead to a variety of conditions whose underlying cause is inflammation. These can include a variety of chronic illnesses, including diabetes, COPD (Chronic Obstructive Pulmonary Disease). Others include high blood pressure.

At the brain level, the vagus nerve will transmit information to the frontal cortex, which is an area responsible for behavior. Its malfunction can, therefore, lead to the development of negative behavior that promotes the progress of a myriad of diseases. These may include symptoms like anxiety, that may evolve into full-blown panic attacks. Others may include deterioration of self-control, which can encourage, for example, overeating. The net impact may be an increase in weight, which would worsen some conditions, including diabetes and hypertension.

The malfunctioning of the right branch of the vagus nerve can harm the heart. Atrial fibrillation can be as a result of the dysfunction.

The imbalance due to the malfunctioning of the vagus nerve can cause the SNS (Sympathetic Nervous System) to result in overworking of the heart leading to cardiac arrest or ischemia.

Vagus nerve dysfunction can also cause insomnia, which is a lack of sleep. The net effect can be an increase in sympathetic activity as the vagus nerve is the one whose role involves resting. A negative feedback loop can occur, with the result being an increase in heart rate and anxiety.

Malfunctioning of the vagus nerve can also result in what is known as vagal syncope. The condition causes one to faint.

The vagus nerve can malfunction due to aging. The effect is the development of a myriad of health challenges. The imbalance due to the malfunction can cause, for example, the SNS (Sympathetic Nervous System) to take over the ANS (Autonomic Nervous System). A malfunctioning vagus nerve equals a dysfunctional ANS (Autonomic Nervous System).

The extensive nature of the branches of the vagus nerve means its dysfunction can lead to a reduction in life quality. The net effect can be a reduction in the need for medication, even as one grows older.

Part of the vagus nerve has a role in the sense of taste in a part of the tongue. Its dysfunction can lead to changes in the capability to taste.

Vagus nerve malfunction can originate from the damage of brain areas that control its roles. The injury to these areas can occur due to a variety of reasons, for example, after a stroke. Tumors can also result in damage to the vagus nerve. Some infectious diseases, either bacterial or viral, can lead to vagus nerve malfunction. Toxins can also lead to vagus nerve malfunction.

It is essential to focus should be on the root cause to deal with the malfunction of the vagus nerve. The dysfunction of the vagus nerve can involve its sensitivity levels. A lack of sensitivity, for example, at the gut level, can result in obesity. The converse is also true. The oversensitivity of the vagus nerve can also lead to extreme weight loss as it affects the satiety signals it transmits to the brain.

At the GIT (Gastrointestinal Tract), vagus nerve dysfunction can cause symptoms like diarrhea and constipation. Such issues have a basis from lack of gastrointestinal motility. The vagal nerve can also become dysfunctional because of the wrong diet.

Another way in which vagus nerve dysfunction can lead to a myriad of chronic conditions is via its role in oxidative stress. Such a state is responsible for several chronic illnesses. Its dysfunction can point to an imbalance whose impact is an increase in the scenarios leading to oxidative stress.

Malfunctioning of the vagus nerve can also lead to an increase in the production of hormones that may hurt the human body, for example, cortisol. Such substances undergo production, for example, during stress. An overproduction of the same can lead to debilitating effects on a variety of organs. Regarding insulin, its dysfunction can promote a decrease in the body's sensitivity to the hormone.

The essential role of the vagus nerve in inflammation can cause its dysfunction to lead to an increase in the pain levels one experiences when suffering from some conditions.

Different pharmaceutical substances can lead to the dysfunction of the vagus nerve. They achieve the same by either mimicking or inhibiting the actions of the vagus nerve.

How to Use the Vagus Nerve to Regenerate Your Body

The extensive distribution of the vagus nerve within your body provides an opportunity for regeneration through simple steps. There are maneuvers that you can try to stimulate the vagus nerve for the varying effects that you may desire. For electrical stimulation of the vagus nerve, it is prudent to involve the skill of a health practitioner. Overstimulation of the vagus nerve can instead lead to dysfunctions within many body organs. Your focus should be achieving the right balance within the ANS (Autonomic Nervous System), of which the vagus nerve is a principal component of the PNS (Parasympathetic Nervous System).

You can utilize the vagus nerve to regenerate your body in terms of weight loss. The vagus nerve has a role in managing satiety, which is the capability to feel full after a meal. Using dietary elements that stimulate it to send messages to the brain, indicating satiety, can help you in achieving weight loss. For example, foods that are high in dietary fats have the capability of stimulating the vagus nerve. The effect may prove beneficial for some classes of IBS (Irritable Bowel Syndrome). The converse is true if your goal is to gain weight.

The vagus nerve can play a role in the modulation of behavior. You can regenerate your mental state by taking advantage of its capabilities. The vagus nerve achieves the change in behavior by its interaction with various parts of the brain, including the frontal cortex. The capacity can be an essential factor, for example, in mood disorders like anxiety and depression. Using the vagus nerve in this manner can be beneficial in dealing with the side effects of negative emotions. These can include factors like a lack of sleep, which may contribute to a generation of a negative feedback loop, leading to the worsening of the initial mental state.

The vagus nerve does play an essential role in the process of inflammation. The process is known as the inflammation reflex. Here, when in balance with the SNS (Sympathetic Nervous System), it leads to a reduction in swelling. The vagus fiber has the capability of reducing the levels of specific biological substances that would otherwise promote the occurrence of inflammation. Such elements are known as pro-inflammatory cytokines. These may include interleukins and TNF (Tumor Necrotic Factor). You can utilize the vagus nerve to manage the symptoms of inflammatory conditions you may be suffering from, including IBS (Inflammatory Bowel Syndrome).

The role of the vagus nerve in oxidative stress is a factor that you can modulate to regenerate your body. Several cases of chronic diseases have oxidative stress as the underlying factor leading to their occurrence.

Working to promote the actions of the vagus nerve can prove to be beneficial in relieving the symptoms of such conditions. You can stimulate the nerve while concomitantly utilizing pharmaceutical agents for a better impact. Advice from health practitioners is essential in achieving the correct balance.

The vagus nerve is the major component of the PNS (Parasympathetic Nervous System), which is part of the ANS (Autonomic Nervous System). The other major component of the system is the SNS (Sympathetic Nervous System). Some conditions, for example, high blood pressure, may have their root cause as the overactivity of the SNS (Sympathetic Nervous System). You may utilize the vagus nerve to recreate a balance between the two systems through the process of VNS (Vagus Nerve Stimulation). The impact should be a counteracting of the SNS (Sympathetic Nervous System) effects. Such interventions can lead to relief from symptoms of an overactive sympathetic nervous system.

At the secretory level, the vagus nerve plays an essential role. Its capabilities allow it to manage the substances a variety of glands produce. These include a hormone known as cortisol, which generates when one is under stress. Its production seems to occur at a higher level in females than in males. The vagus nerve can lead to a decrease in the production of this stress hormone. You can use the vagus nerve through the process of stimulation to regenerate your body by reducing the production levels of such substances. Other hormones that you may modulate in this manner include insulin.

Regeneration of your body via the vagus nerve requires you to stimulate the fiber. The methods for this vary, including physical maneuvers, chemical, pharmaceutical, and electrical stimulation. Physical exercises may not require the guidance of a health practitioner, while the rest of the methods may need you to seek after expert opinion. When choosing the system to use in regenerating your body via the vagus nerve, it is essential to consider the impact of other substances. Such items, for example, drugs, may have an additive or inhibitory effect on your overall goal. Examples of physical maneuvers include splashing your face with cold water.

Holistically speaking, you can use the vagus nerve to regenerate your body by aiming to create a balance within your nervous system. Homeostasis is the name given to such a state. Here, your body systems work synergistically to achieve a healthy mental and physical state. The dysfunction of either of the two schemes would lead to an asymmetry, which can have a myriad of results leading to adverse signs. The right balance will lead to a better quality of life. You can regenerate your body regularly by stimulating your vagus nerve whenever you notice an imbalance.

You can regenerate your body through your vagus nerve by stimulating it via the process of breathing. Here, you aim to reduce your breathing rate to at least half the usual level within every minute. The impact is the development of the feeling of relaxation as the vagus nerve transmits signals to your brain. At the lung level, specifically your bronchioles, the vagus nerve has receptors that allow it to pick up messages for onward transmission.

The overall impact can be a reduction in, for example, your heart rate and, therefore, your blood pressure levels. Such a response can be beneficial when suffering from chronic conditions.

Chapter 10: Physical Exercises for Activating the Vagus Nerve

Activating the vagus nerve can be via a variety of methods, including chemical, electrical, and physical. Each of these ways possesses varying advantages and disadvantages. Chemical processes generally utilize pharmaceuticals to achieve activation of the vagus nerve. Electrical activation of the vagus nerve can involve surgery or can be via the use of non-invasive procedures. The former way requires the presence of a certified health practitioner. Some devices can activate the vagus nerve via the skin in areas where its endings are accessible, for example, behind the ear. There are physical exercises that also can activate the vagus nerve.

The advantage of utilizing physical activities to activate the vagus nerve vary. You may be able to incorporate some physical exercises in your daily routine to achieve activation of the vagus nerve. The simplicity of physical activities can help you maintain the process in the long term, which is an essential component of reaping the benefits. The impact of the activation of the vagus nerve on the human body is usually long-term. It, therefore, requires you to be consistent. Physical activities as tools for vagus nerve activation also help you avoid the side effects of invasive methods of stimulation, including the risk of infections.

One of the physical exercises you can incorporate to activate the vagus nerve is the cold temperature effect. Here, the focus is to lower the temperature of your body. You can achieve the same via a variety of methods, including showering using cold water. You may also choose to dip your face into ice-cold water.

The effect will cause the activation of the vagus nerve as it responds in a bid to maintain homeostasis. Regarding dipping your face into cold water, you can focus on wetting the area between your forehead and the neck.

You can utilize your breathing to activate the vagus nerve. Here, your focus should be to reduce the breathing rate per minute to half its regular pace. The vagus nerve can communicate with the bronchioles within the lungs. The net effect is the development of relaxation. Focus on taking deep breaths. Those with an active vagus nerve, for example, athletes exhibit a slower rate of breathing rate per minute. There are receptors at the bronchiole level that are in communication with the vagus nerve. As your lungs expand during the deep breathing session, the vagus nerve undergoes activation.

Gargling can also promote the activation of the vagus nerve. The basis is the innervation of parts of the throat by the vagus nerve with the process causing the activation. The effect can be via the point of contact of the voice box. The vagus nerve innervates the back of the throat. The temperature of the substance you are gargling should be regular. The vagus nerve interacts within the throat with the muscles of the soft palate, making swishing a viable method to activate the fiber. You can repeat the process regularly to activate your vagus nerve.

Another physical technique that you can utilize to activate your vagus nerve is the Valsalva maneuver. Here, you hold your nostrils between your fingers and close your mouth. You then try to force your breath against the same areas. The result is the activation of the vagus nerve. You can carry out the maneuver while sitting or when in an upright posture. The action will cause an increase in chest pressure, which, in turn, will lead to activation of the vagus nerve. The expulsion of the air against airways that are not open should involve the use of moderate force.

Meditation is another method that you can utilize to activate your vagus nerve. The net impact is the development of a feeling of rest or relaxation. Within the ANS (Autonomic Nervous System), the vagus nerve is responsible for relaxing the body, which may involve encouraging the occurrence of positive moods. You can incorporate the practice of meditation into your regular schedule for maximum benefits. Making a chanting sound can activate your vagus nerve through the movement of the muscles of the vocal cord, an area where the fiber innervates. You can vary the length of the meditation depending on your requirements.

Singing is another method for activating your vagus nerve. The basis is the impact on the vocal cords with the muscles surrounding this area undergoing innervation via the vagus nerve. The process requires you to sing loudly, which works better than humming. The action will cause movement of your vocal cords, therefore, activating the vagus nerve. The method has no restriction in terms of the type of songs to utilize to achieve activation of the vagus nerve. You can incorporate this method into your daily schedule. The benefit of using singing to activate the vagus nerve is the capability to carry out other tasks concomitantly.

Another way of activating your vagus nerve can be via the use of physical exercises. The focus here is achieving the right level of exercising so that the vagus nerve undergoes activation. The preferable kind of physical activity that promotes vagus nerve activation are aerobic exercises. The impact will be a reduction in your levels of stress, which is a function of the vagus nerve as it promotes your body to enter a state of relaxation. Such activity affects HRV (Heart Rate Variability), which is a direct indicator of the state of the vagus nerve.

Laughter is a proven physical exercise that can lead to activation of the vagus nerve. The basis is the movement of the vocal cords as you engage in laughing. In some scenarios, you will employ laughter in a social setting, which will doubly impact your capability to activate your vagus nerve. Such an effect is possible as the environment is presumably one that encourages you to take a position of relaxing, which is a function of the vagus nerve. The action can move you from the point of stress, which is a function of the SNS (Sympathetic Nervous System).

For physical exercises to promote vagus nerve stimulation effectively, it is essential to incorporate these activities regularly. You may, therefore, opt for actions that are simple to incorporate into your daily schedule. Choosing an exercise that allows you to work on other issues simultaneously is preferable. Activities that work with other actions beneficial to the vagus nerve can help you double your impact regarding activating the fiber. The repetitive steps can assist you in taking advantage of the phenomenon of neuroplasticity. Here, regular actions encourage the formation of new thought processes that change your outlook, for example, positively, a factor that can promote activation of your vagus nerve.

A physical pose that you can take to activate your vagus nerve is to focus on lifting your pelvis to a level higher than you face. Your heart level should also be higher than your head. The impact is the activation of what is known as pressure receptors. These have their location at your neck within the carotid arteries. Some refer to them as baroreceptors. Such an action will cause the vagus nerve to receive information that causes it to undergo activation. The fiber, in return, will cause your heart rate to lessen while decreasing the activity level of the SNS (Sympathetic Nervous System).

Manually massaging, for example, specific areas of your neck, can be a physical activity that can lead to the activation of the vagus nerve. Here, the focus is to apply the appropriate amount of pressure. You can preferably carry out the exercise while in a standing position. An area of the neck that can promote the activation of the vagus nerve through massage is the anterior lateral region. Focusing on the areas where the vagus nerve passes through will have a positive effect on your goal of activating the fiber.

Listening to music in comparison to singing can also be a physical exercise that causes the activation of your vagus nerve. The focus here is to engage your mind in music that positively affects your vagus nerve. Music that allows you to reach a mental space of relaxation is preferable. You can incorporate such actions regularly and can take advantage of the process while concomitantly carrying out other vagal stimulating exercises. An example is fusing song in the background as you take bodily poses that encourage activation of the vagus nerve. The impact can double by utilizing such twin actions to activate your vagus nerve.

The physical exercise of learning music can also lead to the activation of your vagus nerve. The phenomenon of neuroplasticity plays a supporting role in such scenarios. Here, your brain forms novel neural pathways as you take the path of learning, for example, new music. You can choose to multitask with singing, an action which is also beneficial in the quest to activate your vagus nerve. You may opt to learn, for example, new genres of music, which will cause the process of vagus nerve activation to occur. The regularity of such actions can play an essential role in activating the vagus nerve.

The specific activity of stretching is a physical exercise that can promote the activation of your vagus nerve. The actions can occur after a session of aerobic exercise or on its own. Regular practice of stretching can cause an increase of HRV (Heart Rate Variability), which is an indicator of the vagal tone. The correlation is proportional to an increase occurring when you undertake stretching regularly. The practice can be gentle on your body, leading you to a place of relaxation, which is a function of the vagus nerve.

Exercising, known as resistance training, can be beneficial as a physical exercise that causes the activation of your vagus nerve. The advantage of such actions is the capability to carry out the activities within your home without necessarily a myriad of equipment. Simple everyday objects, for example, towels, can be beneficial when undertaking resistance training. The gentleness of such activities on the body can cause the activation of the vagus nerve. Such training may also be advantageous to individuals across a broad age set. Those undertaking resistance training can exhibit an increase in HRV (Heart Rate Variability), which is an indicator of how the vagus nerve is functioning.

Another physical exercise that you can incorporate to activate your vagus nerve has its basis as the gag reflex. Here, the posterior section of the pharynx undergoes stimulation, for example, via tactile stimulation. The result is the activation of the vagus nerve. The actual stimulation can occur using a variety of materials, for example, a cotton swab or toothbrush. You can incorporate the exercise via brushing your tongue whenever you brush your teeth. The posterior areas are the ones in communication with the vagus nerve, where the fiber also plays a role in determining taste.

Your sleeping posture can assist you in activating your vagus nerve. Lying on your right side can cause activation of your vagus nerve, even after short periods, for example, five minutes. The action can cause you to relax, a function attributable to the vagus nerve. When opting to use sleeping positions to activate your vagus nerve, it is essential to avoid those poses that have the opposite effect. Sleeping in a supine posture, for example, can cause the activation of the SNS (Sympathetic Nervous System), which can work to negate the PNS (Parasympathetic Nervous System). The vagus nerve is a component of the latter part of the ANS (Autonomic Nervous System).

A simple physical exercise that can promote activation of your vagus nerve is chewing gum. The action can cause tactile stimulation of the posterior part of the pharynx, an area that the vagus nerve innervates. The result can be an activation of the vagus nerve. The advantage of the exercise is the capability to carry it out concomitantly with other actions that lead to the activation of the vagus nerve. Choosing such a pathway can assist you in doubling the impact you have regarding activating the vagus nerve.

Chapter 11: Epilepsy and Vagus Nerve Self Help

The vagus nerve is also known as the tenth (10th) cranial nerve, a name whose basis is its position among the cranial nerves. The numbering starts from the layout at the beginning region of the brain going backward. As with other cranial nerves, it leaves the brain via the brainstem. It consists of two branches known as the left and right vagus nerves. These branches divide to innervate diverse body sections. The extensive nature of its distribution means it plays a central role in the management of different body processes, including at the brain level.

To take advantage of the benefits of the vagus nerve level, it requires stimulation. The process can be via a variety of methods, including electrical, chemical, and manual. The latter manner is ordinarily non-invasive, which may translate to a lower level of side effects. Electrical stimulation of the vagus nerve may require the assistance of a health practitioner as some devices require surgery to place beneath the skin. Some tools are non-invasive and are simple to control, with their use only applicable when necessary. Chemical stimulation may utilize pharmaceutical ingredients that activate the vagus nerve at varying sections of the body.

Stimulation of the vagus nerve can lead to a variety of benefits that are translatable in many disease states, including epilepsy. Its use in epilepsy is now approved. Some individuals who use the method have had a decrease in the number of seizures. Some describe an improvement in the intensity of the seizures with a reduction occurring. Additionally, some individuals report an enhancement in their mood, which can translate to an overall advancement in life quality. Some individuals can use a magnetic device to control the seizures whenever they get a warning of its occurrence. Caretakers can also take control when one is under attack.

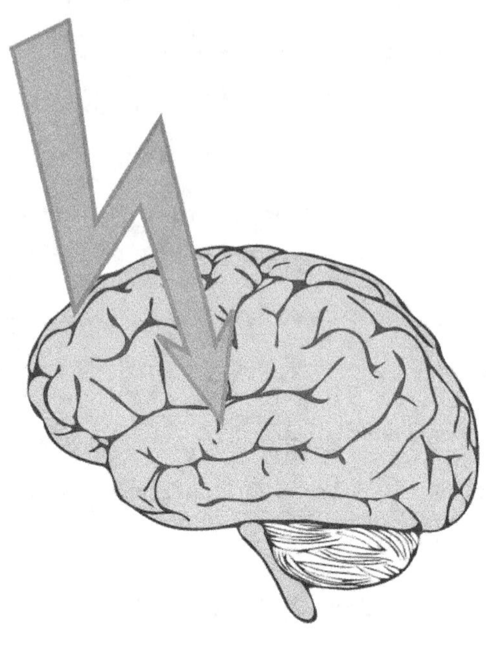

Vagus nerve stimulation works to regulate the electrical activity in the brain, whose irregularity is a foundation for the appearance of epileptic activity. The regulation of such activity inhibits the occurrence of seizures. The vagus nerve in such a scenario transmits electrical pulses to the brain level mildly and regularly. Achieving such regularity is via presetting the intervals for sending signals to the brain. Modifications happen at a single level until the attainment of the appropriate speed. Adjustments occur, taking into account a variety of factors, including the possible concomitant use of, for example, pharmaceutical substances.

The procedure for inserting a device under the skin to stimulate the vagus nerve in epilepsy is usually an out-patient process. Some health practitioners can choose for you to remain overnight, while others will release you within hours. Local or general anesthesia can be in use depending on varying factors. The process may involve an incision at the neck level and below the collar bone. The wires from the device whose insertion is at the region lower than the collar bone undergo wrapping around the vagus nerve at the neck level. The incisions are usually small in size.

The interventions can lead to a myriad of side effects, with some reducing in intensity and even disappearing altogether in a couple of days or weeks. These may include voice hoarseness. In severe cases, the side effects may require the removal of the device entirely. Some individuals may experience difficulty when swallowing, with some experiencing a negative influence on their breathing. Adjusting the particulars of the equipment may cause a relief of the negative symptoms. Other side effects may arise from the procedure of surgery itself, for example, the occurrence of infections or pain at the site of insertion.

The effects of vagal nerve stimulation, for example, in epilepsy, take time before the exhibition. It could take months or even years before an individual notices the changes. Having this reality in mind can help you in being patient with the process. Such periods are also useful for the adjustment of the device to the appropriate levels. The positive effects of the procedure can also potentiate over time. Some individuals end up getting complete relief from the seizures with the use of pharmaceutical substances withdrawn in some cases. Such vagal nerve stimulation can be beneficial in epileptic events that do not respond to the use of conventional medicines.

There is an age limit in the usage of vagal nerve stimulation in epilepsy. Younger individuals, for example, those below twelve years, may not use the procedure for epileptic scenarios. Some regions can allow the use in pediatrics who have tried other conventional medications for epilepsy in vain. Getting information on the effects of the procedure in younger individuals can also prove to be a challenge. The recording of changes in such a population may require varying strategies, for example, carrying out tests that can indicate the brain activity level.

Vagus nerve stimulation in epileptic patients can prove beneficial for individuals who, for example, are unable to utilize conventional treatment schedules. An example is pregnant women. Regular medications for epileptic conditions may have devastating effects on the unborn child. In such scenarios, using, for example, non-invasive methods of vagus stimulation may be the best choice. Those who are unable to undergo surgery may also benefit from non-invasive vagal stimulation. Some individuals also take medications that would negatively interact with conventional drugs that are in use to control epileptic seizures. Those who have undergone surgery to control epilepsy in vain may also benefit from vagal nerve stimulation.

The specific type of seizures one is suffering from is an essential factor in determining whether vagal nerve stimulation will be useful. The focal type of seizures is the one found to benefit the most from vagal nerve stimulation. Improvement can also occur in individuals who experience general kinds of seizures. Your health practitioner will be an essential source of information on whether the procedure will be beneficial to you. Patients undergo comprehensive review before a determination occurs on their suitability to take advantage of vagal nerve stimulation. Such tests should generally occur within a hospital or clinic setting.

The device for vagus stimulation consists of two main parts, including the lead, and the generator. The former segment consists of a wire that moves from, for example, the collar bone to the position of interaction with the vagus nerve. The generator section contains a battery that powers the device. The battery can last for years, with some brands enduring for up to ten (10) years. The wire is flexible and generally consists of lead material. The device uses the interaction point to carry out stimulation to the brain. The tool works like a pacemaker to the head.

Some precautions to take when you undergo the invasive type of vagus stimulation include avoiding MRI (Magnetic Resonance Information) devices. It is essential to let your health practitioner know of any medical interventions you are to undergo when you have the device placed within your body. Discussions regarding, for example, looking to have a baby should take place in advance with your medical practitioner. Some tests may not be harmful but may require adjustments from the point of, for example, the device settings. When traveling, for example, internationally, you may need a note from a certified medical practitioner stating the details of the device fixed within your body.

Vagus nerve stimulation for use in epilepsy usually involves the left branch of the fiber. The activation is at the cervical level. A magnet interacts with the internal device, which one can use to control the tool, for example, when they get a warning of an impending seizure. The lead wire acts as an electrode. The right branch of the vagus nerve fiber is not generally in use because of its link to the heart. Stimulating it may lead to negative consequences, for example, a distortion of the heart function.

Some instances require the activation of the right branch of the vagus nerve. The disadvantage, though, is that unlike the left-wing, its stimulation may not have any effect on depression, a symptom that may occur concomitantly with epilepsy. Its benefits are more suitable for conditions like heart failure. For stimulation of the right vagus nerve, the incisions for implanting the device are on the right side of the chest and the neck regions. The safety element of such stimulation is a factor when health practitioners are deciding on which branch to utilize. Trauma, for example, to the left side of the chest, may cause them to choose to stimulate the right side.

The mode of action that stimulation of the vagus nerve utilizes to control epilepsy is still under debate. Some scientists believe its capability lies in its stimulation of the release of specific biological substances known as neurotransmitters. Others believe its actions have their foundation as the release of electrical impulses, which can interrupt seizures within the brain. Its effects concerning epilepsy follow its link to the head. Some studies are ongoing whose aim is to learn the specific pathways with which the vagus nerve can control epileptic seizures.

Historically, the earliest record of utilizing vagus nerve

stimulation to control epileptic seizures dates back to the year 1883. The medical community at the time did not adapt to this method leading to its abandonment. Its proponents argued that vagal nerve stimulation would promote seizure control by causing the decrease of cerebral blood flow and heart rate. More than fifty (50) years later, the effect of stimulating the vagus nerve on the CNS (Central Nervous System) underwent demonstration in 1938. Vagus nerve stimulation led to the activation of the cerebral cortex, specifically the frontal lobe areas. In 1937, its ability to inhibit motor activity when under the process of stimulation was showcased.

The use of vagal nerve stimulation for epilepsy that does not respond to medication is now global, with over seventy (70) countries approving it for such conditions. Some of the countries that are using VNS (Vagal Nerve Stimulation) for epilepsy include Canada, China, European Union, Japan, and the USA (United States of America). The majority of these regions are utilizing the procedure within all age groups with the USA (United States of America) approving it for those who are twelve (12) years and older. The approval by both the USA (United States of America) and Canada was in

2001.

The cost-effectiveness of VNS (Vagus Nerve Stimulation) for use in epilepsy is dependent on the specific method in use for the procedure. Physical maneuvers generally do not require any gadgets, making it the most affordable option. The challenge, though, is the inability to be specific in the particular areas you want to stimulate regarding the vagus nerve. A lack of specificity can lead to a myriad of side effects, including fainting and hoarseness of voice. Fixation of the device, for example, under the skin for stimulation, will attract surgical expenses.

Each of the branches of the vagus nerve has divisions of A, B, and C fibers. It is essential to consider these differences when setting up the frequency of stimulation for effective control of epileptic seizures through the process of vagal nerve stimulation. A and B are myelinated, while C is not. The latter class makes up the highest percentage of the total amount of vagus nerve fibers. You should also consider the direction of the vagus nerve, with eighty percent (80%) being afferent. Stimulation of the fibers requires varying levels of current. The levels are also dependent on the periods of susceptibility to stimulation.

Given the negative effect of epilepsy on the neural networks of the brain, the importance of vagus nerve stimulation comes into play with its capability to promote neuroplasticity. Such actions can improve cognition in epileptic patients. The process can allow diverse areas of the brain to take over functions of regions whose capabilities undergo compromise whenever an epileptic seizure transpires. You can choose methods that are easy to incorporate into your daily schedule for vagal nerve stimulation to promote health when suffering from epileptic conditions. The focus should be on picking systems that certified health practitioners' support.

Chapter 12: Defeat Anxiety with Vagus Nerve

The vagus nerve is also known as the tenth (10th) cranial nerve, a name whose basis is its positioning relative to other cranial nerves. It works to transmit information to and from the brain, sometimes based on the stimulus it receives from its extensive network throughout the body. At the brain level, it can work through biological substances known as neurotransmitters. It uses such elements, for example, acetylcholine for communication purposes among neurons. It, therefore, has a role in modulating behavioral responses, specifically at the frontal cortex region of the brain. Through such structures, it can affect moods, including anxiety.

The vagus nerve forms the principal part of the PNS (Parasympathetic Nervous System), which is the section of the ANS (Autonomic Nervous System) responsible for getting you into a state of relaxation. The vagus nerve calms you down to achieve the same, which has a positive impact on your overall mental state. The characteristics of anxiety at the physical level may include an increased heart rate, which is a symptom the vagus nerve works to inhibit. In this manner, the vagus nerve will work to deal with both the mental and physical aspects that lead to and come from being anxious.

The vagal tone, which has its measurement as the HRV (Heart Rate Variability), relates to the occurrence of positive emotions. The net impact may be a negation of the feeling of anxiety. An increase in vagal tone may result in a decrease in the exhibition of negative emotions. Various activities can lead to an increase in vagal tone through the process of stimulation. Such scenarios can include involving yourself in physical exercises. A positive feedback loop may develop from such choices, which may inhibit the development of negative emotions like anxiety. Your focus should be incorporating such activities in your schedule regularly.

The vagus nerve plays an essential role in the context of the gut-brain connection. Some individuals, when anxious, may report the feeling of worry within their stomach. Some may even experience a loosening of the stool and stomach aches. The vagus nerve can transmit such information to the brain leading to the development of a negative feedback loop that can worsen the state of anxiety. Increasing the vagal tone by stimulating the vagus nerve can cause these symptoms to disappear. Utilizing vagal nerve stimulation exercises, for example, deep breathing, may work to ease such symptoms.

The emotion of anxiety can arise from a variety of conditions, including PTSD (Post Traumatic Stress Disorder). Low levels of self-esteem can also cause you to develop anxiety, for example, when you find yourself in crowds or socially awkward situations. Your cognitive patterns can also contribute to care by promoting thought processes that lead to an increase in stress levels. Experiencing chaotic events that leave you having no sense of control can also lead to feelings of anxiety. Getting to the root cause of the emotions, in addition to stimulating your vagus nerve, can help alleviate worry.

Vagal nerve stimulation can be a good alternative or an adjunct to conventional treatments for anxiety, which may sometimes lead to polypharmacy. The side effects of such medications may also further complicate the state of anxiety. The impact may include addiction to medicines, which is one of the challenges contributing to the GBD (Global Burden of Disease). Individuals, for example, pregnant women, may benefit from using vagal nerve stimulation to fight anxiety. Such an option can lessen the possibility of the occurrence of, for example, negative consequences on the unborn child. Moreover, some methods of vagal nerve stimulation may be more affordable than conventional routes of managing anxiety.

The role of the vagus nerve in hormone regulation within your body is essential in its capability to fight feelings of anxiety. The stress hormone is known as cortisol, and its production undergoes promotion by the SNS (Sympathetic Nervous System). This part of the ANS (Autonomic Nervous System) also stimulates the creation of the biological substance adrenaline that is suitable for fight or flight scenarios. Stimulation of the vagus nerve can lead to a reduction of both cortisol and adrenaline, allowing your body to become calm, a requirement for getting rid of the feelings of anxiety.

Stimulation of the vagus nerve can promote the production of biological elements that encourage the relaxation of your body. Such substances may include acetylcholine. Others are oxytocin and prolactin. The vagus nerve, when it undergoes stimulation can also cause the release of vasopressin, an element that encourages your body to relax. These substances can work synergistically to prevent tension, which, in turn, can fight any feelings of anxiety that may tend to develop. They have the capability of helping you recover, for example, after facing a stressful situation or experiencing trauma and injury. They are also useful when healing both mentally and physically from illness.

The ability of your vagus nerve to undergo stimulation via physical maneuvers can help you defeat anxiety that stems from a feeling of a lack of control. Some of the activities that stimulate the vagus nerve are simple to initiate, giving you a tool that you can utilize to control the rising of any negative emotions. Practicing some of these maneuvers can create a positive feedback to your cognitive capabilities. The memory of having taken control through the exercises when the feeling of anxiety arose can act as proof of having the mental power you require to relax.

Regular practice and incorporation of such exercises can aid your body in tapping into the power of neuroplasticity, which can further help you defeat anxiety. Here, there is a formation of novel neural pathways within your brain every time you take control of the negative emotions. The phenomenon, therefore, over time, makes it easier for you to deal with anxiety. It allows you to form a new way of thinking. The capability provides you with a different thought framework that you can tap into whenever you face, for example, situations that would previously lead you to develop anxiety.

Part of the reasons for the development of anxiety can be a lack of enough oxygen supply to your brain. The result is a stress response by your body, which can promote the negative emotions of anxiety. Physical maneuvers, like deep breathing, can increase the levels of oxygen concentration, which involve the movement of the diaphragm. The additional effect is the stimulation of the vagus nerve, which has its fibers innervating the lungs. The net impact is the reduction of feelings of anxiety. Such a maneuver is easy to implement whenever you face such situations that lower your oxygen concentration, leaving you feeling anxious.

The capability of vagus nerve stimulation to negate other negative emotions like depression can have a positive impact on reducing feelings of anxiety. Such emotions can sometimes lock in a negative loop fashion. Canceling one can mean the capability to manage the other. Vagal nerve stimulation is now in use to manage depression, particularly the type that does not respond to conventional medications. Breaking the link between negative emotions can be the answer to defeating the feelings of anxiety. Such actions can also improve your cognitive capabilities when handling such emotions.

The extensive distribution of the vagus nerve among various body organs can be a resource for fighting feelings of anxiety. The basis is its capability to cancel the physical symptoms that may relate to worrying. These may include headaches, an increase in heart rate, and sweating. Other signs of anxiety may include fatigue and restlessness. The two-pronged capability of the vagus nerve, that is, physical and mental methods, can be a source of relief from anxiety. As the physical symptoms subside, as you stimulate your vagus nerve, you may get a mental shift. The net impact may make you feel in control, therefore, negating the feelings of anxiety.

The feelings of anxiety have a variety of effects that

may affect your mental or physical state. You may develop an increase in heart rate, which, in turn, can lead to an escalation in blood pressure. The stress hormones that undergo production when you are anxious can promote the breaking down of your immune system. The net impact can be an increase in your susceptibility to infections, which can, in turn, reduce your quality of life. Anxiety can also cause you to break down healthy social relations, which can further worsen your mental state.

Anxiety is an indicator of our bodies that we are out of balance, either physically or emotionally. The key to reinstating the balance is finding out the root cause and then using tools, for example, vagus nerve stimulation to get to the point of positive emotions. Getting to know the reason behind the feelings of anxiety can be a resource that helps you recognize what to avoid to maintain your mental health. You may also develop positive perspectives, for example, becoming empathetic towards those who are undergoing similar situations. Other individuals may learn how to handle anxiety by learning from your journey.

Anxiety may stem from physical causes, including heart

conditions, hyperthyroidism, and medications. Ailments that affect the heart, for example, the mitral valve can lead to feelings of anxiety. Here, the valve does not work correctly, impairing its capability to close. Substances that cause stimulation, for example, amphetamines, caffeine, and cocaine can also promote feelings of anxiety. Some medications, when withdrawn, can lead to the development of anxiety. Having low levels of sugar in your blood, a state known as hypoglycemia, can also cause you to develop feelings of anxiety. Sorting out the conditions can cause feelings of anxiety to dissipate.

You can use the physical maneuver of singing to help you get rid of your feelings of anxiety. The singing should be loud. The action can cause stimulation of the vagus nerve, which has its fibers innervating the muscles of the vocal cords. The result can be a reduction in the feelings of anxiety and the symptoms of the same. Additionally, the act of singing can act as a distraction away from negative thinking patterns that may be driving the feelings of anxiety. The impact of crooning is an increment in HRV (Heart Rate

Variability), which is an indicator of the vagal tone.

Humming can also aid in dissipating the feelings of anxiety. The action has a physical effect on the vocal cords, which is a point of innervation for the vagus nerve. The impact, therefore, is its stimulation, which may lead to a decrease in your feelings of anxiety. Additionally, the action can act to distract you from negative thought processes that may be promoting a negative feedback loop resulting in feelings of anxiety. Humming also has a positive effect on your HRV (Heart Rate Variability). The measurement indicates the state of your vagus nerve.

You can use the vagus nerve to defeat anxiety by encouraging its stimulation through the act of meditation. The action supports the function of the PNS (Parasympathetic Nervous System), of which the vagus nerve is a principal component. Here, you can tap into the power of the phenomenon of neuroplasticity. The impact will be the formation of neural pathways that support the dissipation of anxiety over time. The PNS (Parasympathetic Nervous System) is in charge of getting your body to relax, an essential component of getting rid of feelings of anxiety. Regularly incorporating meditation into your schedule can have significant positive effects on your mental state.

You could also stimulate your vagus nerve to defeat feelings of anxiety via the method of cold treatment. Here, you could opt to take a cold shower or dip your face into ice-cold water. The effect is an increase in the performance of the PNS (Parasympathetic Nervous System) with a concomitant decrease in the actions of the SNS (Sympathetic Nervous System). The overall impact is the increase in the function of the vagus nerve, which will get your mind to relax. The symptoms of anxiety-driven by the SNS (Sympathetic Nervous System) will also dissipate.

Chapter 13: Trauma and Vagus Nerve

The causes of trauma can vary with the impact being either emotional or physical and sometimes affecting both the mind and the body. The emotional scenarios that can lead to injury involve being in chaotic situations, for example, wars, where you lose the ability to control unfolding events. Individuals who have been in war zones may suffer trauma in the form of PTSD (Post Traumatic Stress Disorder). The trigger may have been the horrific scenes they were witnesses to in such regions. Physical trauma can occur, for example, from accidents or even violent experiences.

Varying emotions may accompany trauma, including the feeling of fear. Anxiety may accompany such emotions as your mind starts anticipating the reoccurrence of the situations that primarily led to your negative mental state. You may undergo emotional stress as your subconscious tries to adjust to its new realities. These emotions may form a negative feedback loop, with each of them driving the occurrence of the other. The net impact may be the development of panic attacks that may affect your quality of life. Some individuals may experience paranoia after a traumatic event. Some cases may escalate to mental conditions like schizophrenia if one does not seek help from certified mental health practitioners.

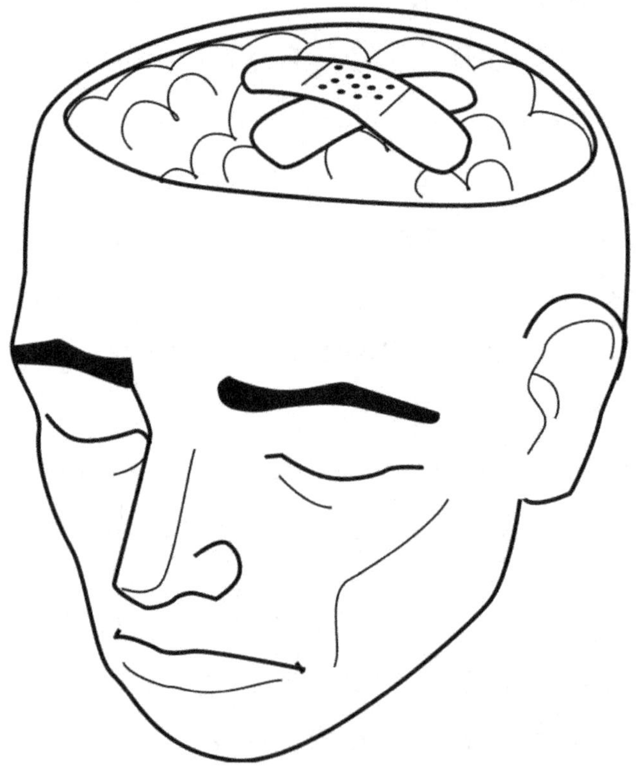

The capabilities of the vagus nerve can prove useful as

a standalone or adjunct to conventional management of trauma, depending on a variety of factors, including the extent of harm suffered. The psychological trauma that does not respond to standard therapy may benefit from stimulation of the vagus nerve. In some cases, the use of VNS (Vagal Nerve Stimulation) can support the reduction of the usage of drugs. The effect is a reduction in the risk of experiencing side effects that may occur from drug usage. The advantage may be essential in populations that are more sensitive, for example, pregnant women.

Trauma that has an underlying cause of inflammation or that results in the same may benefit from vagal nerve stimulation. The nerve fiber has an essential role in the phenomenon known as the inflammatory reflex. Here, it works to reduce the production of biological substances that promote the occurrence of inflammation. Examples of such elements include TNF (Tumor Necrotic Factor) and Interleukins. Utilizing the capacity of the vagus nerve in this manner may provide relief to physical trauma, which, in turn, may improve your life quality. The net impact may be a reduction in psychological trauma due to a reduction in the levels of pain as the extent of inflammation decreases.

The vagus nerve has a distinct function in how we manage our emotions, for example, through our social interactions. One of the ways how the vagus nerve can undergo stimulation is via the process of laughing. The action causes the muscles surrounding your vocal cords to move to result in the stimulation of the vagus nerve. Psychologically, particularly in a healthy social setup, the impact of laughing can be a source of stress release. The net effect may be healing from emotional trauma.

In extensive physical trauma, the vagus nerve can prove useful due to its innervation of many organs. Stimulating it can concomitantly lead to relief in various areas of the body. It runs from the brain stem, innervating organs within the neck, chest, and abdomen. These include the vocal cords, the tongue, and the lungs. Its branches also innervate the heart and the digestive system. The vagus nerve also interacts with a variety of glands, including the pituitary, hypothalamus, and pancreas. Its interaction with the digestive system exhibits in the gut-brain axis, which is an essential connection within the human body.

Trauma that results in depression may benefit from vagal nerve stimulation. Studies show that the vagus nerve can promote healing in despair, particularly the types that do not respond to conventional treatment. Some individuals experience complete healing from depression when they undergo vagal nerve stimulation. The effect of the stimulation generally takes time, with improvement occurring in months or even years after the start of the treatment. Vagal nerve stimulation can also be in use concomitantly with conventional treatments for depression. The impact, may over time result in a reduction in the dosage of the drugs.

In the context of trauma, working on improving your vagal tone, a state whose measurement is via the HRV (Heart Rate Variability), can prove to be useful in your healing journey. HRV (Heart Rate Variability) is an indicator of the vagal tone of the nerve. It improves via a variety of actions, including physical exercise. The effect of physical activity can lead to the production of biological substances, which may have a positive impact on your mental state. The net result may be a reduction in the anxiety and stress whose foundation is trauma. Such elements are known as endorphins.

Imbalance of the functioning of the vagus nerve can, by itself, be the basis for the occurrence of trauma. The extensive distribution of the vagus nerve within the human body means its dysfunction can lead to both mental and physical injury. In such scenarios, the goal of vagus nerve stimulation can be to recalibrate the fiber to a healthy state. A loss of vagus nerve sensitivity can result in a pronouncement of the SNS (Sympathetic Nervous System) portion of the ANS (Autonomic Nervous System). Such an imbalance can worsen trauma, for example, by increasing the occurrence of inflammation.

Recalibrating the vagus nerve in traumatic conditions can be via invasive or non-invasive methods. The choice is dependent on a variety of factors, including the extent of the trauma experienced. Non-invasive methods tend to have fewer side effects, unlike invasive options. The latter may cause you to be susceptible to infections as it involves surgery, albeit minor. Other side effects of VNS (Vagus Nerve Stimulation) include experiencing voice hoarseness. The impact of such stimulation may reduce over time. Some scenarios require the use of both methods to attain adequate response that will lead to healing over time. Such decisions are case dependent.

Oversensitivity of the vagus nerve can also lead to trauma, both physical and mental. A condition known as vagal syncope can occur from the overstimulation of the vagus nerve. Here, one experiences fainting due to the oversensitivity of the vagus nerve to a variety of triggers. The trigger may be of an emotional form, for example, experiencing extreme levels of fear. Some may experience the same, for example, when they see blood. The experience may result in the formation of a negative feedback loop due to, for example, the negative emotions that may accompany such an episode.

The connecting role of the vagus nerve between the brain and the gut can be beneficial for the trauma that relates to eating disorders. The kind of foods you eat can play a role in determining how you react to emotional situations. Some foods promote the functioning of the vagus nerve, while others diminish its activity. The vagus nerve is also known to play a role in your ability to feel full, a process known as satiety. Its capacity within the gut-brain axis can prove useful in introducing foods that can aid in healing trauma, both physical and mental. Its stimulation may also promote healing from conditions raising incidents of emotional eating.

The vagus nerve can prove to be useful in scenarios where the origin of trauma is the presence of an overactive SNS (Sympathetic Nervous System). The system is part of the ANS (Autonomic Nervous System), whose other component is the PNS (Parasympathetic Nervous System). The vagus nerve makes up the principal portion of the PNS (Parasympathetic Nervous System). In a healthy subject, these two systems are in balance, a state known as homeostasis. These systems work in opposite directions having effects that balance out each other. Some of the results of an overactive SNS (Sympathetic Nervous System) include an increase in heart rate and, therefore, a rise in blood pressure levels.

Physical and emotional trauma may interrelate with the latter leading to physical manifestations. Some individuals who have undergone, for example, emotional trauma due to abuse, may exhibit physical symptoms. These include experiencing COPD (Chronic Obstructive Pulmonary Disease), IHD (Ischemic Heart Disease), and liver disease. Others may get STDs (Sexually Transmitted Diseases), for example, due to promiscuous behavior, whose underlying reason is emotional trauma. The connecting role of the vagus nerve between your mind and body can prove useful in handling such scenarios.

The role of the vagus nerve in memory plays an essential role in how you handle trauma, both emotional and physical. Its stimulation can improve specific types of thought. The vagus nerve can promote reinforcing of some memories. Stimulation of the vagus nerve can also lead to a diminishing of some considerations, including those relating to fear. The basis of such an impact is the release of specific biological substances when the vagus nerve undergoes stimulation. Such elements counteract the activity of the components that lead to an increase in negative emotions like fear. An example of an ingredient that undergoes production during the reaction of fear is adrenaline, whose production occurs via the SNS (Sympathetic Nervous System).

Trauma to the vagus nerve, for example, due to the process of vagotomy, can hurt your ability to heal from traumatic events. Historically, those suffering from PUD (Peptic Ulcer Disease) underwent such procedures. Trauma, for example, through an accident, can result in dysfunction of the vagus nerve. The principal consequence of such an impact can be the incapacity to absorb Vitamin B12. The deficiency, in turn, can lead to dysfunction of nerves, which may result in a negative feedback loop that results in emotional trauma.

The role of the vagus nerve in the phenomenon of neuroplasticity can prove beneficial in handling cases of psychological trauma. The phenom allows your brain to find new ways of managing its regular functions. It, therefore, supports the improvement of cognitive function, which is the foundation for providing new frameworks for your thinking processes. In some cases, trauma links to memories, whose basis is your thought patterns. Stimulating the vagus nerve can, therefore, provide you with the capacity to form new thought patterns to link to the traumatic memories. Such actions may provide a route for the release of psychological stress.

Stimulation of the vagus nerve for relief from trauma may require involving a certified health practitioner. Psychological trauma can include multiple issues that demand a balance in approach. It may require the use of vagus nerve stimulation in conjunction with conventional psychological treatment options. Achieving the right level of VNS (Vagal Nerve Stimulation) is essential to have the impact desired. Stepwise stimulation of the vagus nerve may prove necessary in the pursuit of the right level of fiber excitement. Examples of conventional therapies that are in use for psychological trauma include talk therapy.

Vagal nerve stimulation may prove useful in trauma that results in anxiety. The symptom of an increase in heart rate in such situations has its foundation as the activity from the SNS (Sympathetic Nervous System). Stimulating the vagus nerve can result in a reduction in heart rate, which would alleviate the symptom of anxiety arising from the trauma. Such an impact can result in the formation of a positive feedback loop as one realizes relief from such effects. Overstimulation of the vagus nerve in such situations can cause the heart to stop beating, a fatal action. The goal is achieving the right level of vagal nerve stimulation.

Vagus nerve stimulation can have the effect of increasing your desire to involve yourself in social situations. Its capability to drive your body and mind into a state of relaxation may be the basis for the same. Such interactions, when healthy, may provide a route for release of stress that arises from trauma. The communications may alleviate episodes of depression. Listening to other individuals, in social settings, for example, in support groups, speaking about their experiences can reduce the feeling of loneliness that may exhibit due to psychological trauma. Vagus nerve stimulation is, therefore, an essential component of handling trauma, both physical and emotional.

Chapter 14: Frequently Asked Questions

What Is the Vagus Nerve?

The vagus nerve is also known as the tenth (10th) cranial nerve. The reference is an indicator of its position relative to other cranial nerves, which number thirteen (13) in total. It consists of two branches, that is, the left and the right vagus nerves. It leaves the cranial section via the brain stem. The vagus nerve then moves down to the neck, chest, and abdomen. It works to innervate several body organs. It can, therefore, connect the body organs to the brain. In terms of length, this nerve is the longest of the cranial fibers.

How Does the Vagus Nerve Work?

The vagus nerve is a component of what is known as the PNS (Parasympathetic Nervous System). It constitutes the more significant portion accounting for eighty (80) percent of the same. The PNS

(Parasympathetic Nervous System), in combination with the SNS (Sympathetic Nervous System), constitutes the ANS (Autonomic Nervous System). The vagus nerve works to transmit information from diverse body organs to the brain. It also sends messages from the head to the areas it innervates. It accomplishes the same via a variety of methods, including promoting the production of different biological substances.

What Is the Effect of Stimulating the Vagus Nerve?

VNS (Vagus Nerve Stimulation) can result in a myriad of effects, given its extensive distribution throughout the human body. The process can impact both your mental state and your physical body. The vagus nerve, being part of the PNS (Parasympathetic Nervous System), will promote a feeling of relaxation when it undergoes stimulation. At the organ level, these effects may include a decrease in heart rate, a reduction in your breathing rate, and the promotion of the movement of food through your GIT (Gastrointestinal Tract). It may also promote or inhibit the production of biological substances from several glands.

How Can One Stimulate the Vagus Nerve?

The main ways to stimulate the vagus nerve are through chemical, electrical, and physical maneuvers. Synthetic stimulation of the vagus nerve can be via the use of pharmaceutical substances that mimic the effects and actions of the nerve fiber. Electrical stimulation involves the use of devices that undergo placement around the vagus nerve. The procedure may require surgery, or one can opt for non-invasive methods. Physical maneuvers that can result in stimulation of the vagus nerve include practicing deep breathing, gargling, humming, singing, and meditation.

Is It Advisable to Stimulate the Vagus Nerve While on Medication?

The indications for VNS (Vagus Nerve Stimulation) involve its use in situations that do not respond to conventional medication. Based on the advice of a certified health practitioner, VNS (Vagus Nerve

Stimulation) may be in use concomitantly with drugs. The expert will consider how the effects of VNS (Vagus Nerve Stimulation) will interact with the medications you may be using. In some scenarios, the use of VNS (Vagus Nerve Stimulation) may allow for a reduction in the dosage in the use of conventional medication. The expert in healthcare will make such adjustments dependent on a case-to-case scenario.

How Long Does It Take to See the Impact of VNS (Vagal Nerve Stimulation)?

The impact of VNS (Vagal Nerve Stimulation) is dependent on a variety of factors. Generally, it takes months, even years, for one to feel its impact. The key is to work closely with your certified health practitioner to determine whether you are benefitting from the process. In the initial stages, there may be a need for adjustments to the frequency of stimulation. The act of getting the correct balance may define the time between the introduction of the inducement and the consequent exhibition of its effects.

What, If Any, Are the Side Effects of VNS (Vagus Nerve Stimulation)?

As with other interventions, VNS (Vagus Nerve Stimulation) may result in a variety of side effects. Such symptoms usually occur in the first few days after the procedure. Over time, such effects ordinarily diminish. Apart from the regular side effects, the invasive type of VNS (Vagus Nerve Stimulation) may attract negative impact that associate with surgical interventions. These may include outcomes like infections and pain at the sites of incisions. Other effects of VNS (Vagus Nerve Stimulation) may constitute hoarseness of voice and alteration in taste capabilities.

What Is the Minimum Age Limit for Using VNS (Vagus Nerve Stimulation)?

The age limits for the use of VNS (Vagus Nerve Stimulation) differ depending on the regulatory authority in charge of healthcare within varying jurisdictions. In some countries, the minimum age at which an individual can undergo VNS (Vagus Nerve

Stimulation) is twelve (12) years. Other nations allow for its utilization within the pediatric population. The supervisory role of their use may lie in the expertise of health practitioners across jurisdictions. It is preferable to work with certified health professionals to determine the suitability of the procedure on a case-to-case basis.

Can Stimulation of the Vagus Nerve Aid in Relieving Anxiety?

At the brain level, the vagus nerve promotes the production of the biological substance known as acetylcholine. The element is a type of product that allows for communication between neurons. It, therefore, is a neurotransmitter. The other component of the ANS (Autonomic Nervous System) that is the SNS (Sympathetic Nervous System) promotes the production of adrenaline. Here, the neurotransmitter results in the fight or flight response that can result in anxiety. Acetylcholine instead inhibits such a reaction leading to relief from worry.

Is VNS (Vagus Nerve Stimulation) Beneficial in Depression?

VNS (Vagus Nerve Stimulation) can prove itself useful in some cases of depression, particularly the ones that are not responsive to conventional medications. Several countries are allowing their application as a concurrent option to the use of traditional drugs. Some population segments unable to utilize such medication may benefit from the use of VNS (Vagus Nerve Stimulation) to address depressive episodes. Examples may include pregnant women or those who have previously undergone some types of surgery. Some individuals report an improvement from symptoms of depression after utilizing VNS (Vagus Nerve Stimulation), with an enhancement in their moods.

Can VNS (Vagus Nerve Stimulation) Be Beneficial in Epilepsy?

The vagus nerve is a cranial nerve that connects to diverse organs within the human body. Some studies show its stimulation may prove beneficial in epileptic conditions. Its impact is principally two-fold, with its effectiveness improving the frequency and extent of seizures. Some patients using VNS (Vagus Nerve Stimulation) to manage seizures report an improvement in their moods and, therefore, their quality of life. Some jurisdictions approve the use of the technique for the management of epileptic conditions that do not respond to conventional treatment.

What Are Some of the Conditions in Which VNS (Vagal Nerve Stimulation) Is Contra Indicatory?

As with other medical interventions, there are conditions in which it is improper to institute VNS (Vagal Nerve Stimulation) as a form of management for disease conditions. The preferable approach is to hold discussions with certified health practitioners who are experts in the technique. They can offer advice on a case-to-case basis while considering the details of the medical condition in question. Those who have undergone the procedure of vagotomy, where the vagus nerve is, for example, cut may not benefit from the technique of VNS (Vagal Nerve Stimulation).

What Does the Invasive Type of VNS (Vagus Nerve Stimulation) Entail?

VNS (Vagus Nerve Stimulation) that requires the insertion of a device below the skin is known as invasive VNS (Vagus Nerve Stimulation). Here, two incisions at the position below the collarbone and the neck provide areas for VNS (Vagus Nerve Stimulation). The generator section has its location at the area below the collarbone and connects with a lead wire that wraps around the vagus nerve at the cervical segment. A battery forms part of the generator, therefore, powering it to function. These elements work in conjunction with a magnet whose utilization can calibrate how the equipment works.

What, If Any, Are the Precautions That One with the Implanted Device for VNS (Vagus Nerve Stimulation) Should Take?

As with other medical interventions, it is essential to consider the interactions of this intervention with external factors that may, for example, change the function of the device responsible for VNS (Vagus Nerve Stimulation). Magnetic equipment may alter how the tool works. Medical interventions like MRI (Magnetic Resonance Imaging) can affect its functioning. Before deciding to undertake any medical test, you should discuss the possible impact with certified health practitioners who are knowledgeable about the procedure and its consequences.

What Are Some of the Conditions That Can Benefit from VNS (Vagus Nerve Stimulation)?

The extensive distribution of the vagus nerve throughout the human body can make its stimulation beneficial to diverse medical conditions. Such conditions can either be mental or physical. Its connective capability between the body organs and the mind can make it useful for conditions consisting of both components. Some ailments that may profit from VNS (Vagus Nerve Stimulation) include anxiety, depression, and IBS (Inflammatory Bowel Syndrome). Others are heart disease, auto-immune conditions, and migraines. VNS (Vagus Nerve Stimulation) may also be beneficial in cases of fibromyalgia, tinnitus, which is ringing in the ears, and thyroid disorders.

How Long Does Surgery to Implant the Device for VNS (Vagal Nerve Stimulation) Take?

The length of time taken to undergo surgery to implant devices for VNS (Vagus Nerve Stimulation) depend on a variety of factors. Different medical jurisdictions have their standards for how long the procedure should take. Generally, the intervention should take hours with discharge within the same day. Some health practitioners may opt to keep you longer to follow your response to the insertion of the VNS (Vagal Nerve Stimulation) device.

How Long Does the Battery Within the Generator of the VNS (Vagal Nerve Stimulation) Device Last?

The devices that assist in VNS (Vagal Nerve Stimulation) differ in the model and, therefore, capabilities. Some batteries can last for a few years, with some functioning for more than half a decade. External factors may also affect the length of time that the elements operate. These may include the altering of their operating capabilities, for example, by exposure to substances that inhibit their functioning. Samples may include vulnerability to devices through magnetic impact. Physical trauma to the areas where the elements are within the body can also alter how long the batteries can survive.

What Is the Use of the Magnet Given After the VNS (Vagus Nerve Stimulation) Surgery?

After the surgery to implant the VNS (Vagus Nerve Stimulation) device, your health practitioner may hand over to you a magnetic device. The tool may be useful in calibrating the functioning of the vagus nerve. Some scenarios may call for calibration, for example, when you experience an aura, which is an indicator of, for example, the beginnings of an epileptic attack. Your caretaker may also use it to assist you once you are under a seizure attack.

Is It Okay to Travel with the Implanted VNS (Vagal Nerve Stimulation) Device?

In most cases, the implantation of the VNS (Vagus Nerve Stimulation) device should not affect your regular travel. The precautions may involve keeping away from equipment that has a magnetic impact, as these may alter the functioning of the tool. You may preferably carry documentation that shows you have undergone implantation of the VNS (Vagus Nerve Stimulation) device. Such proof may prove critical, for example, when traveling internationally or when passing through airports, the latter where checking may need explanation. Do not forget to carry the magnet in case you may need to use it.

Can I Undergo Surgery While Having the VNS (Vagus Nerve Stimulation) Device Implanted?

Some medical interventions may result in negative consequences when you have undergone implantation of the VNS (Vagus Nerve Stimulation) devices. Your health practitioner will consider the repercussions of the same and advise you accordingly. The essential point is to let your doctor know of your history for them to make the right decision. Some surgeries may require the inactivation of the VNS (Vagus Nerve Stimulation) device to ensure the health of your body.

Conclusion

Thank you for making it through to the end of *Vagus Nerve: Activate Your Natural Healing Ability with Self Help Power Exercises to Overcome Anxiety, Retrain Your Brain and Overcome Chronic Illness, Depression, Trauma and Start to Improve Your Life*, let's hope it was informative and able to provide you with all of the tools you need to achieve your goals whatever they may be.

The next step is to practice stimulating your nerve using the exercises in the book to start your journey of reaping the benefits of vagus nerve stimulation. Before doing so, consult with your certified health practitioner to ensure the activities are beneficial and safe for you. Incorporate the exercises into your schedule to ensure consistency, which is the foundation of reaping the benefits maximally. Look out for opportunities to practice the techniques to get better at handling anxiety, chronic illness, depression, and trauma.

Aim to take advantage of the different techniques to personalize the activity that has the most significant impact on your road to recovery. This journey of discovery can also help you choose the exercise that will be easiest for you to implement, for example, at short notice. Evaluating all the activities through practice will also provide you with diverse frameworks for stimulating your nerve that may be suitable for a myriad of situations. Going through all the exercises will, therefore, give you a sense of control over varying scenarios. With practice, you should be able to get faster relief from stimulating your nerve.

It is best to incorporate these techniques in a stepwise manner to be sure which one had the most noticeable impact. Doing so will help you eliminate exercises that do not align with your recovery on this journey of self-healing.

Finally, if you found this book useful in any way, a review on Amazon is always appreciated!